MY FAMILY
IN THE
GREAT WAR

MY FAMILY
IN THE
GREAT WAR

Edward F Malet de Carteret

Reveille
PRESS

Reveille Press is an imprint of
Tommies Guides Military Booksellers & Publishers

PO BOX 3229
Eastbourne
BN21 9RZ

www.tommiesguides.co.uk

First published in Great Britain by
Reveille Press 2014
Reprinted 2021

For more information please visit
www.reveillepress.com

ISBN 978-1-908336-46-0

Printed and bound in the UK

Contents

Dedication

For all those gallant men and women who
made the supreme sacrifice for the British
and Allied cause in the Great War

Their Names Liveth For Evermore

Preface

THE task of putting this publication together has been a long labour of love going back over the past 25 years or so. This was probably the date when in my mid twenties I started to become fascinated by the exploits of my family members who had taken part in the Great War. Midshipman Philip Malet de Carteret and Captain Harold Ackroyd were early features in my conscience. I saw Philip's portrait, which used to hang in the dining room (formerly the 'catroom' our sitting room), almost daily during the 1980's and 1990's whilst I lived in our family house, St Ouen's Manor. It is very special to be able to read through Harold's Red Album, which contains his letters and photographs and resides in the Library. Philip has a blue box with his 'life' in it and I probably only really started looking through its contents it in the mid 1990's. John (Jock) Armstrong came into my life much later on, probably only fully since the beginning of the new Millennium, and I have been greatly helped in his story by his son, the recently late, Professor David Armstrong and his wife Jenny in Sydney to whom I offer my most sincere thanks. I am so sorry that David has not lived to see the fruits of our labours.

In a peculiar way my late father Philip never seemed to talk to any of us much about our more immediate family members, although I do know he was fiercely proud of them all. It is difficult to tell these stories in a dispassionate way their being my kin and it is also hard to really get completely inside their skins, particularly as, naturally, I never met any of them. In reality, there is not much to go on other than their letters, photographs, medals, family speak and the relatively few third party accounts that we have. Nevertheless, we can build up a picture in our minds of two certainly young, athletic and intelligent boys in both Philip and Jock's case, and a loving husband and father in Harold, and indeed a very fine intellect.

Philip only saw his parents and his Jersey family manor house home on holidays from school and college during the years 1907-14. Most sadly, he saw them only once during his whole time of service from the outbreak of the war – 10 days of leave in May 1916, just before his death at Jutland.

We know, though, that he was fully aware of the manor's significance and he probably had some inkling as to the role and responsibility he would have had in later life when, as the eldest son, he would have inherited the Fief Haubert, which includes the manor house. Jock would never again have seen Philip when the family left Australia in 1907. It's fun to imagine them playing together as small children on Bondi Bay! I find it tragic that Jock spent several of his leaves in Jersey at St Ouen's Manor in 1918 seeing his Aunt and cousins but without seeing Philip.

I do know that Reginald, Philip's father, was devastated at his loss and that my grandfather, Guy, the 2nd son, never filled his large shoes. Harold Ackroyd comes into our family story after the Great War when his daughter, Ursula, my grandmother, married Guy in Malvern in 1930. But there we have them; my great-uncle, my 1st cousin twice removed and my great-grandfather all on the paternal side of my family.

I would just like to finish this brief piece by adding my thanks to those who have helped and encouraged me over the years into finally getting this humble effort into print. First of all, to my cousin Christopher Ackroyd for his lasting interest and friendship and for his permission to reproduce his grandfather Harold's condolence letters and photographs. I must acknowledge that he is the co-author of the chapter/story of Harold Ackroyd and he is tireless in his promotion of him. To my late father Philip for his long time support and to my elder brother Charlie, for his generous help and permission to publish the family archives of both Philip and Harold held at St Ouen's Manor. To my younger brother, Bob, and sister, Liz, for their continuing help and support. My friends, Warwick Blench, and fellow WW1 author, Ian Ronayne. Barrie Bertram and all my friends in the Channel Islands Great War Study Group (www.greatwarci.net). Capt Pete Starling of the Army Medical Services Museum, Ash Vale, Aldershot. Nigel Steel at the Imperial War Museum, Col (Rtd) Graham Parker, Jo Legg, all my friends in the Western Front Association, Brain Best, Iain Stewart, Tom Johnson BEM, Jim Carlo and all my friends in the Victoria Cross Society. David Saunders and Foster Summerson in the Gallipoli Association.

My grateful thanks go to the Department of Photographs at the Imperial War Museum for their kind permission to reproduce several photographs and to the National Library of Australia, Canberra (John Malet Amstrong – MS9675), for their permission for the reproduction of Jock Armstrong's letters and photographs.

Finally, I would like to thank my 16 year old daughter, Anna, whom I hope will one day come to appreciate the exploits of her illustrious ancestors.

Ned Malet de Carteret
Jersey, December 2020

Midshipman Philip Reginald Malet de Carteret (1898-1916)

AT 4.26pm on 31st May, 1916, a terrific explosion occurred on the British battlecruiser, HMS Queen Mary, at the beginning of one of the greatest modern sea battles of the 20th century – Jutland. One and a half minutes later, the ship sank with a compliment of 1,266 officers and crew, of which there were nine survivors. Philip Malet de Carteret was sadly not one of them.

Born in Sydney, Australia, on 23rd January 1898, Philip was the eldest son of Jurat Reginald Malet de Carteret (1865-1935), Seigneur of St. Ouen's Manor in Jersey. He was educated at Ebor Preparatory School in Lausanne in 1907 and Mr Rhodes, Mottingham. After this he attended Eltham College, before entering RNC Osborne in 1911. He took first prize in French on leaving for RNC Dartmouth in 1913 to take his Midshipman's course.

Philip in Uniform – date unknown (CMdeC)

His father, Reginald, a lawyer, had left Jersey for Australia and married there in 1895. His wife was the New Zealand born, Amy Anne

RNC Osborne, Grenville Term, December 1912 (Mrs E. Dickson)

Armstrong, his second cousin, (1865-1950), daughter of Capt Richard Ramsay Armstrong (Jersey born) who narrowly missed winning a Victoria Cross at the taking of the Redan at Sevastopol during the Crimea War. Philip's siblings were equally born in Sydney – his elder sister, Ella Marie (Ellie/Elley), had been born in 1896 and his younger brother, Guy (my grandfather), was born in 1901.

Philip was a keen sportsman. His fifty-four surviving letters written during the Great War constantly narrate sporting events – swimming,

HMS Canopus (C MdeC)

Philip on HMS Canopus, 1914 (?)
(CMdeC)

hockey matches and tennis. He wrote thirty-seven letters to his father, fifteen to Guy and two to Elizabeth (Grandma). Seven were written prior to 1914.

At the outbreak of the war, he was passed out as Midshipman on 4th August, 1914, and was posted to HMS Canopus. Canopus was a pre-war dreadnought, which was commissioned in 1899. She was originally built for service in China, but didn't get past Aden on her maiden voyage due to engine troubles. Canopus was due to attain a speed of seventeen knots. The ship displaced 12,950 tons and her armour consisted of four 12-inch guns with an approximate range of 12,000 yards and twelve 6-inch guns. When he joined the ship it was under the command of Captain Heathcote S. Grant (later Admiral, Sir).

Canopus was at first patrolling in the North Atlantic, when she was ordered to assist the South Atlantic Battle Squadron of Admiral Sir Christopher G.F.M. Cradock. The ship arrived in Port Stanley on the 18th October.

Cradock was ready to leave to pursue the German Squadron under Graf von Spee, but dismayed to learn that Canopus would have to stay in port for at least five days to clean her boilers and repair an engine defect. Captain Grant told the Admiral that even after the repairs the ship would only be capable of twelve knots (1).

The squadron left Port Stanley on 22nd October, its top speed being eighteen knots, that of the slowest ship, Otranto. While the Canopus was coaling, Captain Grant discovered that his chief engineer, Commander William Denbow, had been mentally ill for some time and had deliberately falsified his reports about the state of the engines. According to a report by the junior engineering officer, Lt. Commander Sydney Hart, Denbow had never left his cabin once during the whole voyage and so could not possibly have inspected the engines. It turned out that after a minor repair, the ship was capable of approaching the seventeen knots she had made on her sea trials after recommissioning. The unfortunate engineer was sent back to England under medical attention. He was invalided out of the navy.

Postcard from Port Stanley, October 20th, 1914 (C MdeC)

Captain Grant did not want to break W/T silence to tell Cradock the news (2).

Canopus left for the Magellan straits on 23rd October to join the rest of the British squadron, which consisted of three old armoured cruisers (Good Hope – the flagship, two 9.2-inch modern guns with a range of 13,500 yards and sixteen 6-inch guns), Monmouth (fourteen 6-inch guns) and Cornwall. The rest of the squadron consisted of Glasgow (two modern 6-inch, ten 4-inch guns) and Bristol, with two light cruisers and the armed merchant cruisers Otranto, Macedonia and Orama.

Cradock's ships were far inferior in both firepower and age to Graf von Spee's squadron which consisted of the two modern cruisers; the Scharnhorst (twelve 8.2-inch guns that had a range of 13,500 yards and also 5.9 inch guns with a range of 11,000 yards) and Gneisenau (twelve 8.2-inch guns) both of which had sailed from the China Sea to the South Pacific, together with three light cruisers; the Leipzig (ten 4.1-inch guns with a range of 11,500 yards), Dresden and Nurnberg. Their vessels were capable of 23 knots.

The German officers and crew numbered some two thousand two hundred. They were seasoned professionals in the main and had served together for over a year. The vast majority of the British crews on the other hand had been civilians less than six month previously.

THE BATTLE OF CORONEL

The Battle of Coronel (off the coast of Chile) took place on 1st November. Winston Churchill, the First Lord of the Admiralty, was convinced that Cradock had orders not to engage the Germans without the protection of Canopus. However, Canopus was slow and although she was steaming towards the British fleet at fifteen knots, Craddock thought she was travelling at twelve and a half knots. She had two colliers with her.

At 6.18pm, Craddock increased his speed to seventeen knots and radioed Canopus with a message "I am going to attack the enemy", although the German ships were beyond his range. Captain Grant signalled back that he still had two hundred and fifty miles to go before he could reach Cradock's position (3).

At 7.00pm, the Germans opened fire at a range of 12,000 yards (seven miles). The Scharnhorst hit the Good Hope with its third salvo and rendered the fore 9.2-inch gun useless. It continued to fire four salvoes a minute. By 7.23pm the range was 6,600 yards. At 7.50pm, the Good Hope, which had been hit between thirty and forty times, was shattered by an explosion that produced a column of flame rising over two hundred feet above her decks. (4)

Canopus had intercepted a message from Glasgow to the Good Hope reporting the enemy in sight. She increased to full speed and dispatched her colliers to Juan Fernandez and headed northwards in the hope that she would arrive in time to engage the enemy. At about 9.00pm she received a signal from Glasgow that it was feared that the Good Hope and Monmouth were lost and the fleet scattered. Canopus turned around, picked up her colliers and made back for the Magellan Straits via Smyth's channel, probably the first battleship to make use of them, a great navigational credit to her. (5)

Admiral Cradock perished along with 1,600 fellow officers and ratings.

Rear-Admiral Archibald P. Stoddart was now in command in the South Atlantic, on HMS Carnarvon, and he decided to go south to Montevideo to meet the remainder of the scattered fleet.

On the 6th November, Canopus was back in the Falklands but was ordered to go to Montevideo. Half way on her journey she was recalled and arrived back in Port Stanley on the afternoon of the 7th November. Canopus could not get a reply from the wireless station in Stanley and thought that the harbour had been captured by the Germans. The islanders in turn thought that they were the enemy. The island had at that time a population of about one thousand, mainly Scottish crofters.

To protect the wireless station, Canopus entered the inner harbour at Port Stanley and forced herself aground on the muddy bottom, and moored taut head and stern in a position that would enable her to command the southern approach. Top masts were housed, and the ship, masts and funnels were painted all colours of the rainbow in great big sploges to render her less visible. A look-out station was set up in Sparrow Cove and three 12-pounder batteries were hastily constructed to dominate the approaches (6)

LETTER TO REGINALD OF 4TH DECEMBER 1914 (PUBLISHED IN "THE MORNING POST" 21/01/1915)

"My Dear Dad,
I wish you a very happy Christmas! We are still in the Falkland Islands and are organising a proper defence in case the enemy meditate an attack. The only thing worth having is the wireless station, which is valuable to us as it is the only British Wireless Station in these parts.

You have doubtless seen in the papers all about the German armed merchantman, "Kaiser Wilhelm der Grosse" being sunk by our cruiser "Highflyer". Well we had been specially sent out to the North Sea to sink her, but before we got there, we found our work had been done for us by the, "Highflyer". We were frightfully sick.

Do you remember seeing about a midshipman on the "Cressy" who saved 87 lives (or thereabouts) including that of his commander, when the "Cressy" "Houge" and "Aboukir" went down. His name was Cazalet. Well he was a chap in our term who had mobilised with us at Dartmouth. Of course we were very glad to see it although we were sorry to see the list of the drowned midshipmen whom were in our term also. Talking of drowned people, eight people were drowned here while crossing a creek in a punt three days ago. The punt capsized, and none of them could swim so they were all drowned.

They were not men from the ship, but from the shore. They grappled, dredged and dived for their dead bodies and succeeded in recovering seven. I had to convey them to the Town in my boat. It was pretty ghastly work!

Although the Canopus seems to have taken but a small part in the war yet she has really done more than any other ship hereabouts, and a good deal more than most ships in the Navy, for although we have not fought an action, yet we have kept all the trade routes clear and unmolested and frightened away any marauding German armed merchantmen or cruisers, that might have been skulking around.

*We have run the ship hard and fast on to the mud (on purpose) so it
looks as if we were going to stay here till the end of the war – whenever
that will be.*

*Our poor dilapidated engines have at least got a rest after tramping
up and down the Atlantic and Pacific Oceans for weeks on end with
scarcely an interval.*

I hope everyone at home is quite fit and well
With love to all from your affectionate son
Philip"

After the defeat at Coronel, The First Sea Lord, Lord Fisher acted
swiftly. He ordered the immediate release of three battlecruisers to serve
in the Atlantic, two to go to the Falklands, HMS Invincible and HMS
Inflexible and one, HMS Princess Royal to the West Indies to guard
the Panama canal. On 7th December the battlecruisers arrived in Port
Stanley with Vice-Admiral Sir Frederick Doveton Sturdee flying his flag
in Invincible as Admiral of the Squadron. His orders were to annihilate
Von Spee's squadron.

THE BATTLE OF THE FALKLAND ISLANDS

December 8th was to prove an exception to the rule in the Falklands where
it usually rains for 21 days during the last month of the year, for it was a
perfect mid-summers day as the fleet was coaling in harbour.

*At 7.56am the Glasgow fired a gun to attract the attention of Invincible
who was busy coaling, that Canopus had reported smoke in sight to the
south. At 8.15am a signal came from the flagship to "raise steam for
full speed, report when ready" (7)*

*The enemy's two leading ships Gneisenau and Nurnberg were in
sight approaching the wireless station. When they were near Wolf Rocks
they stopped engines and turned north-eastward. Canopus opened fire
over the low neck of land at 9.20am with her 12 inch guns, firing five
rounds at a range of 12,000 yards. Hoisting their colours,*

The enemy turned away to the S.E. to join the main squadron. (8)

*From survivors it appears that one of Canopus's shells had
ricocheted, striking the Gneisenau at the base of her after funnel. It
was also claimed that a piece of another hit the Nurnberg. (9)*

*At 9.45 the British squadron weighed and proceed from harbour,
the last of whom cleared by 10.30am. Glasgow came out first, followed
by the two battlecruisers doing 25 knots, followed by Kent, Carnarvon
and Cornwall doing about 22 knots.*

The Admiral reduced speed for an hour to 20 knots at 11.15am to allow the "County" cruisers to catch up. At 12.47 he hoisted the signal "Open fire" and eight minutes later the Inflexible fired the first round of the battle at the Leipzig. The Invincible followed almost immediately after. Both ships were going their full speed, nearly 27 knots and firing at a range of 16,000 yards (over 9 land miles). (10)

The fight between the two British battlecruisers and the German cruisers lasted 6 hours. The Scharnhorst sank at 4.17pm and the Gneisenau heeled over at 5.45pm. Invincible had been hit about 22 times, 18 directly and had a list to port as two shells had struck below the waterline. The Wardroom had been demolished. There had been no casualties amongst her crew of 950 men. The Inflexible had 2 hits, I crew killed and three wounded. The British squadron in total lost 7 men killed and 18 wounded (3 subsequently died). The Germans lost 2,260 men, including Von Spee and his two sons, Lt's Heinrich and Otto. The Dresden was the only ship to escape the battle and was later sunk on 14th March, 1915 by the Kent and Glasgow.

Vice-Admiral Sturdee was rewarded with a baronetcy.

LETTER OF 9th DECEMBER, 1914

"After the action off the Chilean coast, we sent home word for reinforcements. These did not arrive until the day before yesterday, when a large fleet came here comprising the, "Invincible", "Inflexible", "Carnarvon", "Cornwall","Kent","Glasgow" and"Bristol". Up to this time we had heard nothing of the Germans. The very next day (yesterday), the whole fleet of Germans, which had been in the action of November 1st – Scharnhorst, Gneisenau, Leipzig, Dresden and Nurnberg – turned up. They couldn't have come at a more opportune moment, as if they had arrived earlier our fleet would not have been here and if they had arrived later the fleet (which was to have left today) would have gone!

We, the Canopus went to General Quarters about 10.00am and opened fire with our 12 inch guns. Our other ships could do nothing, as the land was between them and the enemy, and most of them were coaling. We fired a lot of shots and hit the "Gneisenau". By this time the fleet had weighed and were coming out at full speed. The Germans turned tail and fled with the fleet at full speed after them.

Of course we could not follow as we were on the mud. Still we had opened up the action, prevented the enemy from shelling the Wireless station and saved the fleet from being attacked while at anchor. All that day we waited anxiously for news. Towards evening we got the welcome news that the "Invincible" and "Inflexible" had sunk the "Gneisenau" and "Scharnhorst". Later we heard that the "Leipzig" was on fire fore and aft and she sank soon after. Then the signal came through from the "Kent" "Have sunk the Nurnberg". We were frantic with joy. We have got a lot of prisoners on board. The officers are being kept in the Captain's lobby, where they are guarded by sentries with fixed bayonets. They get quite respectable food, however! The men are all forrard. One prisoner who can talk English told us they had intended to destroy the wireless station, to land by night and sack the town and sink all the colliers and store-ships in the harbour, sink the "Canopus" if we made any resistance and decamp to West Africa taking the crew of the "Canopus" with them. There was only one thing they didn't know all about and that was the arrival of our fleet.

If the fleet had arrived only two days earlier or two days later, it would have been all up with us and everyone else on the Falkland Islands.

However it turned out all right. I am only sorry we were not able to go out and settle some of them ourselves, but anyhow we could not have kept up with the fleet.

Still we did our little lot. "

1915
Transfer to the Dardanelles and the Gallipoli Campaign

HMS Canopus now had orders to go to Malta on 23rd January and it reached there on 8th February having stopped off in Gibraltar. By the 27th it was at Tenedos and ready to start its actions in bombarding the Dardanelles straits.

LETTER TO REGINALD – 6TH MARCH, 1915 PUBLISHED IN "THE MORNING TIMES" 3rd APRIL, 1915

The Falkland Islands WW1 Memorial (Mrs L. Roberts)

"My Dear Dad,
I wish you many happy returns of the day. I hope this letter will arrive more or less on the right date, but of course one can't choose one's own time for letter writing nowadays – one takes one's chance.

We have been having an exciting time lately. After leaving Malta, we went up to the Dardanelles where there are heaps of other ships bombarding the place. We have made a base of a small island just outside the entrance and take turns to bombard.

The other day it was our turn. We went up about 10 miles, past all the forts which have already been silenced, till we came to those which had not. It was our business to silence "No 8" fort, which is on the European side. We opened fire on it, and got the range pretty quickly, and then kept on firing with our 6 inch guns and an occasional shot from our 12 inch, it was not until 1 ½ hours after the start that the fort thought of returning our fire, but when they did so they were pretty accurate. They bought our main topmast down, made a large hole in the quarterdeck, the shot going through and damaging the Ward Room, a hole was made in our after funnel, besides the damage done by splinters of shell (they had been firing shrapnel) which I found on the Quarterdeck after the action. Anyhow we went on firing till sunset, which was about 6 o'clock, and then we chucked it in having silenced the fort.

Next day we went along the Asiatic coast outside the Dardanelles hunting for hidden field guns and things which might open fire if we attempted to land men or anything. We rooted out several and silenced then with our 6 inch – blew most of them into the air since we were at such close range. Today we were mostly employed in watching where the shots from the big ships went who were firing overland, and correcting their range for them since they could not see- we fired a few desultory shots ourselves." P.

March 20th-24th. My time was fully occupied at Tenedos as S.N.O. (the Chief of Staff being away with the Admiral at Mudros), re-organising the mine-sweepers, most of whose R.N.V.R. crews had been sent home. the boats being now manned with volunteers, R.N. officers and men, with some R.N.R.

We had already sent a number of men and some officers, volunteers for the minesweeping work, and Lieut. Donohue and Mid. de Carteret, P.O. Heath and Signalman Watkins had done some excellent work in trawler 224 on the worst nights of the sweeping. Mid. Durrant with P.O.'s Soloman and Deadman, A.B.'s Seaman Rooke, Stevens, Blew, Harrod, Sennett and Sexton, with Stoker Green, had been employed under Lieut. Robinson in one of the picket boats directing the sweepers; reports from their commanding officers showed that they had all done well. (11)

Captain Heathcote Grant became Rear-Admiral on 4th June, 1916 and was awarded the CB.

LETTER TO GUY OF 2nd MAY, 1915

"My Dear Guy,
I may as well tell you about the lucky accident, which resulted my getting a slight scratch, which I proudly call a "wound". I was sitting in my boat, which was alongside the pontoon on the beach waiting for the wounded to come along.
Shrapnel was bursting all round us, several in fact, got into the boat. I was hit on the head by a shrapnel bullet and started bleeding like a pig. Luckily the thing was spent, and so, after being bandaged up at a field ambulance place, I was quite all right."

In his copy of "Gallipoli" by John Masefield, Reginald has annotated a mark on page 48:

"The boatmen and beach working- parties were the unsung heroes of that landing. The boatmen came in with their tows, under fire, waited with them under intense and concentrated fire of every kind until they were unloaded and then shoved off, and put slowly back for more, and then came back again." (12)

Philip on his lighter off Anzac Cove, April 1915 (C MdeC)

HMS Canopus camouflaged off Mudros (IWM – Q 73424)

LETTER IN MAY, 1915 TO REGINALD

"My Dear Dad,

The submarine scare turned out to be quite a justifiable one after all. Several times we heard that there was one in the neighbourhood, whereupon we had closed all the water-tight doors (which meant that the Gunroom is inaccessible) and steamed about in circles keeping a sharp look out but it was not until yesterday that we actually saw the effects of it. The flap started at 7.30am, so we were away all the forenoon. We were off Gaba Tepe at the time, but we were expecting to be relieved by the Vengeance some time during the forenoon after which we were going to Mudros to coal and ammunition. At about 10.00am we sighted the Vengeance coming along to relieve us, but when she was about 5 miles away she suddenly altered course, and appeared to be steaming away from us. We wondered what was up, but presently she signalled to us that she had sighted a submarine and fired a torpedo at her, which had barely missed. The scare immediately got worse, and all ships which were anchored, weighed, and we were all cruising about independently. By that time, the Vengeance was close to us, but our Captain being the senior N.O. out there, shifted over to the Vengeance, while we cleared out for Mudros without him and with a destroyer escort.

At 12.30, I was standing on the Quarterdeck with several other people, when someone shouted "They've bagged the Triumph" we all looked at her through our glasses (we were about 4 miles away) and saw her heeled over at an angle of 60 degrees. She was actually struck at 12.26 and soon sank after 12.30. All the torpedo craft and trawlers immediately dashed to her aid and about 700 survivors were picked up, which was very good work indeed, as it means that very few people were lost.

Still, it is a very great disaster, as besides the loss to the navy, one has to consider the effect it will have on the Turks bucking them up considerably .In fact some Turkish officers who were captured said that the Turks would have chucked up the sponge long ago had it not been for the sinking of the Irrisistable, Ocean and Bouvet on March 18th.

The Triumph was a pre-dreadnought battleship, a sister ship to the Swiftsure both of which were purchased by us from Chile. She carried 4 10 inch guns and 14 7.5 inch beside several smaller ones. The Swiftsure is also out here. The Triumph was engaged in the capture of Tsing-Tao at the beginning of the war, and had not been home for 3 years, so it was especially hard luck for the people of those who were drowned.

I think the Canopus is about the luckiest ship in the service (touch wood) whenever a disaster occurs we always seem either to miss it or to clear out just in time e.g 1) off the coast of Brazil where we were nearly torpedoed by the Karlsruhe 2) missing the Coronel Action 3) Admiral Sturdee's fleet turned up just in time to save us from Von Spee at the Falkland Islands. 4) Missing the T.B., which sank the Goliath, by 10

Officers of HMS Canopus in Malta, May 1915. Philip is front row 1st left. Robert Kirk Dickson is front row 4th left (Mrs E. Dickson)

minutes. 5) Missing the submarine, which sunk the Triumph by a hair's breath. Still we are not out of the wood yet.

> *With much love to you all*
> *Your affectionate son*
> *Philip"*

SUVLA BAY
LETTER OF 21ST OCTOBER, 1915 – TO REGINALD

"My dead Dad,

I got ashore this afternoon much to my astonishment. Apparently the Commander has either forgotten that my leave is stopped or else he has compassion on me in my loneliness; anyhow he let me go. We did not go very far (of course one is not allowed up to the trenches unless in khaki) but stayed with the beach master at C beach who is an RNR Lieutenant who used to be in the Canopus. He gave us tea and we gave him newspapers, he took us to his various dug-outs which are very sumptuous as he is in command of the whole peninsular on the southern side of Suvla Bay and therefore a great personage. We yarned the time away, and he sent us back in his own picket boat together with several pieces of shells etc. in the way of curios. We had intended to search in the area of the Great Salt Lake for old shells or bayonets and also climb Chocolate hill, but as we did not do so today we will have to leave it for some other time. I am going to appease the commander with the cartridge-case of an 18 ponder field gun which I brought off today – it may work wonders in the leave line.

The night before last was a fearfully rough night – of course it was my turn for the patrol. It was much too rough for patrol, so we simply tied up to one of the buoys of the gate and showed a light whenever a ship wanted to get in or out. Only the Glory, a destroyer and a trawler wished to go either in or out, so we spent all the night in a miserable condition, rolling and pitching like anything, with the seas breaking green over us incessantly.

Of course it was impossible to get any sleep even in the stern cabin as the water came in over there and soaked us through. At 5 a.m. it became so bad that the senior officer ordered us back to the ship as we were in danger of being swamped.

Winter has begun to set in properly here and we have got fires lit both in the wardroom and the Gunroom. I always pity the military in winter-time- they must have a thin time of it in the trenches what with the cold and wet while we live in comparative comfort in the ships. The other day I was in a picket boat about a half mile off W beach when the Turks, realizing I suppose what a chance they had of wiping out one of the most promising young officers in the British Navy, sung a shell across which pitched in the water about 20 yards from us. Whether it was meant for the beach or for the trawlers, it would have been a pretty bad shot for either, anyhow it was quite close enough to us for my liking. Last night at 11.15pm a stoker expired in his hammock quite suddenly.

They had a post-mortem examination this morning and came to the conclusion it was from heart-failure that he died. Anyhow he was buried at sea from a trawler at 10.30 this morning.

Love to all from Philip."

After the failure of the Suvla action, the campaign was called to a halt and by the end of October Lord Kitchener came out to Gallipoli and recommended its evacuation. The harsh winter set in. The scorching summer had produced thousands of casualties owing to the flies and dysentery. In the freezing snows of the winter, nearly 16,000 troops were evacuated because of frostbite. All Allied forces were evacuated in the famous withdrawal by the end of the year. British and Commonwealth casualties amounted to 115,000 killed and 90,000 evacuated sick. Turkish casualties were in the region of 250,000.

1916

In the early part of 1916 Canopus was involved in patrolling off the Gulf of Smyrna.

In March 1916, Philip was posted for a short time to HMGG Mary Rose, one of five motor gun boats. The flotilla was commanded by Commander M. Smart RNVR in the California. The other members were Penelope, Anzac and Dorothea. Philip's boat was commanded by Henry Ralph Kimber of the Royal Marine Artillery. They were based at Long Island.

Until quite recently I had been ignorant that Philip came home to Jersey on his first and only leave of the war from 5th until 12th May, 1916, just before Jutland. Sadly there is no mention of this in his subsequent letter home.

On May 17th Philip was appointed to HM. Queen Mary. He swapped ships with Midshipman Jan Kent, who went on to be a Commander in WW2 and subsequently a Jersey resident and friend of my parents and grandparents.

Philip departing St Helier on SS Ibex, 5th May, 1916, presumably taken by Reginald. (C MdeC)

HMS QUEEN MARY

The ship was launched in 1912 and completed in 1913.

She had a displacement of 27,000 tons and had a capacity of 75,000 ship horse power giving her a speed of 28 knots.

Her armour consisted of:

8x 13.5-inch guns

16x 4-inch guns

2 x torpedo tubes

She was commanded by Captain Cecil Prowse.

HMS Queen Mary (IWM – Q39898)

HMS Queen Mary in Rosyth. Philip's last letter home to Reginald

HMS Queen Mary
c/o GPO London
May 27th 1916

"My dear Dad
How did the tennis party go off on Monday? I hope you had fine weather. I only wish to goodness I had been there. Although the weather is quite decent here of course it is nothing like as warm as you are having it over there. I was speaking to a chap from one of the ships round here and he said that when his old ship – the Carnarvon – paid off he and all the other snotties got seven weeks leave – seven weeks just think of it! I think that must have been an oversight on the part of their Lord Commissioners of the Admiralty.

Goddard is now permanently back in the Service. He is endeavouring at present to purchase a second-hand motor-bike for as little as he can. He already possesses one which is at present in London but which he is trying to sell and so he is trying to get hold of another one which he will be able to use here and which will come in awfully handy as we are about seven miles from Edinburgh.

I got ashore the other day lured me along to Gieve's where I purchased numerous article of clothing including a mack. Edinburgh isn't half a bad place, anyhow it is better than Metylene. The Scotch people talk in a most extraordinary sort of way that it is quite hard to understand them sometimes.

A company runs large motor-buses from the landing stage into Edinburgh which takes you there in about 20 minutes at an outlay of a bob. If you miss the bus however you can always go by train. You ought to see the scrum for the last bus leaving Edinburgh for Dalmeny. It is simply packed with NO's. Ordinarily built to convey 34 including driver and conductress, the last one I went in contained 67! They were hanging on anywhere, packed like sardines in a tin while the company raked in the shekels.

The Queen Mary is the most up to date ship. Among the many luxuries are a bath room with hot water constantly laid on and two long baths. Also a cinema show to which I went last Thursday and it was quite decent. The Gunroom is well above the water line (in the Canopus you could scarcely have the scuttles open at sea for fear of the water coming in) and contains a gramophone and a pianola. There are 25 of us in the gunroom including 2 subs, an Engineer sub and two clerks. All the rest are snotties, some junior and some senior to us.

We played a game of hockey the other day against the Wardroom. As a matter of fact the wardroom couldn't raise a team by themselves so we made it commissioned officers v junior officers. That meant both our subs played against us. Even then we licked them 4-3 after a very good game. All the wardroom are a very sporting crowd and rag about like anything.

Have Mr and Mrs Le Maistre left Jersey for England? Because a snotty here got a letter from a pal in Oxfordshire saying that he had met a certain Mr and Mrs Le Maistre who asked him if he knew me. I wonder if it could be Mr and Mrs Frank Le Maistre whom Ellie and I dined the other day.

No admirals have come cringing round to me yet although I have seen several since being here. However I live in hopes.

My chest and trunk arrived quite happily the same day as I did. Considering the amount of buffeting they had had they were in quite good condition the only damage being a hinge knocked off my Parallel Ruler box, my sextant was happily intact due to the careful way I had padded it with old clothes.

Has Guy's gramophone been mended yet? They seem to be taking their time about it. Tell us all the news when you write back. Are you able to get plenty of tennis? How are the gooseberries and other fruit getting on? I suppose Jack has left to join his ship again.

Hoping you are quite well, with much love from your affectionate son. Philip."

Extract from 'The Times' June 9th, 1916 regarding the Battle of Jutland.

TIGER IN THE FIGHT
HOW THE QUEEN MARY WENT DOWN

One of the gunners of H.M.S. Tiger, the latest vessel of the British Battle Cruiser Squadron, has given the following account of the battle of Horn reef:

The Lion which was leading the line, followed by the Tiger, Princess Royal, and the Queen Mary, was the first to open fire, the range being about 18,000 yards, and common shell being used. Range-finding continued for a few minutes, neither squadron doing what might be called really good shooting till then.

Then it could be seen that each of the British battlecruisers had begun business in earnest. Control firing was adopted, the speed of each salvo being remarkable. The Germans, too began to get the range as the vessels drew towards each other, and a particularly lucky shot cut away part of the Indefatigable's fire control.

About 4 0'clock every man in the British battlecruiser squadron, each vessel of which had been singling out an opposing vessel, realised that the Germans not only had a preponderance of guns, but more than double the number of vessels. They were clever in realising their superiority. They began concentrating their fire, and every gun of the German Squadron was first turned on the Lion, but hardly a shell hit her. Two asphyxiating projectiles fell on her upper deck behind the bridge, but the majority fell short, sending up terrific volumes of water.

GUNS CONCENTRATED ON THE QUEEN MARY

The two squadrons approached each other for about 20 minutes, and then the enemy suddenly bore away to port, soon turning completely as if they were breaking off action. We turned as well, and manoeuvring continued for 15 minutes, when the German squadron again came ahead, their guns being concentrated on the Queen Mary. They had been poking about for range for some minutes without effect, when suddenly a most remarkable thing happened. Every shell that the Germans threw seemed suddenly to strike the battlecruiser at once. It was as if a whirlwind was smashing a forest down, and reminded me very much of the rending that is heard when a big vessel is launched and the stays are being smashed.

The Queen Mary seemed to roll, slowly to starboard, her mast and funnels gone, and with a huge hole in her side. She listed again, the hole disappeared beneath the water, which rushed into her, and turned her completely over. A minute and a half and all that could be seen of the Queen Mary was her keel, and then that disappeared.

Standing beside Admiral Beatty on the Lion during this awful spectacle of the destruction was his Flag Captain E.M. Chatfield. We both turned around in time to see the unpleasant spectacle... Beatty turned to me and said, "There seems to be something wrong with our bloody ships today" whether the destruction was caused by inadequate armour or poor flash protection in the magazine will never be established.

The German Official History says that the Queen Mary's masts and funnels were distinctly observed by several ships to fall inwards. While smoke and flames issued from the hull, and the former rose to 2000ft, at times completely obscuring Tiger and New Zealand. The Seydlitz reported a small outbreak of fire in the Queen Mary shortly before she blew up, which was thought to be an ammunition fire as noticed in other ships. The

Derfflinger's official report notes that a dense black smoke cloud rose to several hundred yards without a considerable development of flame and in the after gunnery control a particularly violent explosion was seen to the right of the smoke cloud from the Queen Mary at a time given as 1630, and this presumably was the final explosion in her sinking.

HMS Queen Mary blowing up (IWM – SP 1708)

The timetable of events seems as follows; (13)

1) Several hits up to about 1615 from Seydlitz. Apparently including a hit in the after 4 in battery and perhaps another hit near "X" turret. Possibly serious damage in the after 4in battery, including ammunition fire noticed by the Sedylitz.

2) About 1621, hit on right side of "Q" turret and right gun out of action - from Defflinger.

3) 1626, hit on "A" or "B" turret or barbette from Derfflinger and perhaps on left gun of "Q" turret. Explosion somewhere in "A" or "B" shook the ship and hydraulic pressure failed in turrets. Immediately afterwards "A" and "B" magazines exploded. Forepart of ship broken off near foremast and probably destroyed completely. "Q" and "X" turrets wrecked, with cordite fire in "Q" working chamber.

4) After part of ship listing heavily, stern in the air and propellers still revolving.

5) As heel increased, an explosion blew up remainder of the ship.

Extract from a letter by Midshipman J.L. Storey – on of the 9 survivors of the Queen Mary from a compliment of 1,266
5th June, 1916

"*Poor Malet de Carteret who was with me in the Canopus all this time is also gone. I feel it dreadfully. We had been together 6 years all told.*

…. The actual fight was something like this. We left Rosyth on Tuesday evening and steamed towards the Danish coast. At about 3.50 we sounded off,"Exercise action", and all went to our turrets and tested through everything. We were then told that A & Q turret crews could go and get their tea. Q was my turret, the one amidships in the waist between the funnels. At 4.24"Action" was sounded and we all went to our stations, and at twenty minutes to five the order was given "Load all Guns" we all then realised that the real thing had come at last. At 7 minutes to 5 we opened fire at 8 ¾ miles range at the third ship in the enemy's line, and everything went beautifully until 5.21 when Q turret was hit by a big shell, and the right gun put out of action. We continued firing with the left gun for two or three minutes, and then a most awful explosion took place which broke the ship in two by the foremast, it was I believe a torpedo into one of the fore-turret magazines. When the explosion took place, our left gun broke off outside the turret at the rear and fell into the working chamber: the right gun also slid down. The turret was filled with flying metal, and several men were killed. A lot of cordite caught fire below me and blazed up, and several people were gassed.

The men left and myself got to the ladder leading out of the turret and climbed quickly out. There was no panic or shouting at all, the men were splendid heroes. Just as I got out of the turret and climbed over the funnels and masts which were lying behind the turret, and had got off my coat and our shoes, another awful explosion occurred, blowing me into the water, – and the remaining part of the ship, – the after-part blew up. X turret magazine going off.

However eventually we got to Rosyth at 8pm on Thursday."

It is interesting to note that either his memory or watch was wrong by 1 hour?

A letter of 26th June, 1916 to Philip's father Reginald from Bertram G Falle (who later became Lord Portsea), tells of his visiting Midshipman Jocelyn Storey.

25.6.16
9 Clarence Parade
Southsea

"My dear decarteret,

I have today talked with young Midshipman Storey – a nice boy – who was saved from the Queen Mary – He had known your Philip for 6 years and of course speaks feelingly and affectionately of him – he says your boy was in A turret – the first to go – and that it was all over in seconds – there could have been no suffering, indeed there could have been no knowledge of what was happening.

He thinks a shell entered the turret magazine and turret B followed and he thinks a torpedo broke the ship in half, and as his half sank he was thrown into the sea. He found some wreckage off which one of our TGb's, passing at speed, soaked him and the same thing happened a 2nd time after which a 3rd TGb's rescued him.

His clothes had to be cut off him – the explosion of the magazines had generated some gasses which made stiff board of his clothes. He's a brave lad – and his parents say that his nerve has not suffered, but we think he shows some of the effects.

He had a month's holiday or something of the kind.

I feel you will like to have these facts – its something to know there was no suffering. He tells me too of the end of the Black Prince commanded by a real friend of ours – also a question of bad luck?

The Storey's live here – 14 Clarence Parade.

Yours sincerely
Bertram G Falle

Letter of Condolence, 27th June, 1916

HMS. Queen

"Dear Mr & Mrs Malet de Carteret

Just a very short line to express my sincerest sympathy for you all. It must have been a most dreadful blow and I can assure you all that you are not alone in your sorrow. He spent quite a considerable time in the London with us all and most of the senior officers, as well as ourselves, remember him well and have expressed their regret that "such a promising officer" should have been lost.

Everybody has remarked from time to time how calmly he went about his work even under the most trying conditions and more especially at the time when he was wounded at the Dardanelles, when his first thought was for the men under his charge.

I am also sure that when his ship went down, although we can obtain no details, he met his death as a true British officer and gentleman.

Yours very sincerely

Midshipman E Oloff de Wet"

Eric Oloff de Wet was born in Stepney on February 28th, 1897. Eldest son of Captain Thomas Oloff de Wet and Elizabeth Bradstreet. He passed out from Dartmouth in 1914 with the 2nd highest marks. He was awarded the DSC for outstanding bravery in landing Anzac troops at Gallipoli. MID, he was promoted Sub-Lieutenant and subsequently Flag-Lieutenant. On 12th January 1918, Eric was lost at sea while serving on board the M Class destroyer HMS Narborough. Together with her sister destroyer, HMS Opal, they were wrecked on the Pentaland Skerries after running aground in fog. There was only one survivor out of 188 officers and crew. Admiral Mark Kerr wrote a letter to his parents saying "Had he survived he would have become the youngest British Admiral" From "Familie de Wet – HC (Henk) de Wet." The family was living in Jersey during the War.

Dennis G.L. Goddard and Humphrey M.L. Durrant who are mentioned in Philip's letters also died on HMS Queen Mary.

Mid. Humphrey Durrant (Google)

A total of 10 of the boys of the Grenville Term from RNC Osborne served on HMS Canopus with Philip. The other 9 were:

Midshipman Richard TraversYoung. – later Commander, OBE – died 1970's ?

Midshipman C. Burge.

Midshipman Jocelyn Latham Storey. – survived Jutland on HMS Queen Mary.

Midshipman Humphrey M.L. Durrant. – died of wounds on 6/6/1916

Midshipman R H.L. Orde.

Midshipman Robert Kirk Dickson. – later Rear-Admiral in WW2

Midshipman B R.. Cockrane. – Transfer to HMS President. Died 14/3/1919

Midshipman L.H.P. Henderson.

Midshipman L.H.V. Booth.

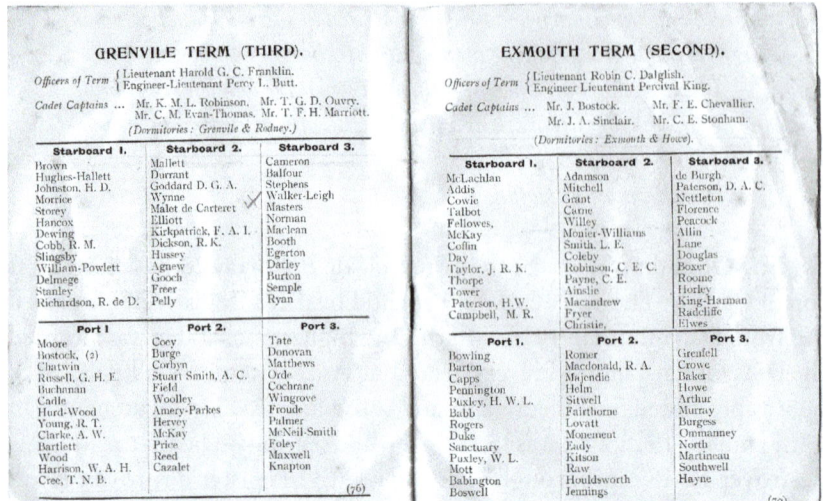

RNC Osborne Roll – Sept 1911, Grenville Term (C MdeC)

POSTSCRIPT

I am in contact with the families of Robert Kirk Dickson and Humphrey Durrant. Robert Dickson's younger brother Archibald William (Archie) served I believe all the war on HMS Queen Mary as a Midshipman and was killed with Philip. Robert's letters are in the National Library of Scotland. Their parents used to go every year to the River Forth at Rosyth and lay a wreath in the river in memory of their lost son. Many years ago I visited HMS Belfast in London. I very much imagine that the fore gun turret of that ship is similar to that of "A" turret of HMS Queen Mary. At least it gives you a good idea of the size of it and of the claustrophobia that I felt inside. I visited Portsmouth for the first time in September 2018 and laid a poppy cross to Philip on the Royal Navy memorial on Southsea Common. I made a memorable trip to Gallipoli in 2003 with a group led by the historian Martin Middlebrook and whilst I did not get a chance to take a boat up the Dardanelles to look at Fort 8, I hope to do so one day.

Oil portrait (C MdeC)

In 2000 a group of divers lead by Innes McCartney discovered and dived on the wrecks of HMS Invincible, Queen Mary, Black Price and Lutzow

Philip's Medals (author/C MdeC)

Stained Glass Window, Grouville Church, Jersey given by Ellie (author)

and this can be seen on his DVD available from www.persicopepublishing. com. I would dearly love to be above the spot where the Queen Mary sank on 31st May, 2016!

An ebook of Philip's letters has been published in 2014 by Mark Tanner and you can also view a copy of these writings at www.greatwarci.net – under Naval Matters. Philip is also remembered by a brass plaque in St Ouen's Church and on the Parish War Memorial. His name is inscribed on the memorial to those without a grave on the Portsmouth Naval Memorial.

Aerial Shot, St Ouen's Manor – early 1980's (author)

References/Sources:

Graf Spee's Raiders – Keith Yates – Leo Cooper – 1995

Notes 1) p133, 2) p 134, 3) p139, 4) p139-41,

The Battle of the Falkland Islands – Commander H. Spencer-Cooper – Cassell & Co – 1919

Ref 5) p 58, 6) p85-86, 7) p87, 8) p89, 9) p89, 10) p90-93

(11) The History of HMS Canopus - Captain Heathcote Grant -The Naval Review – http://www.naval-review.org/

(12) Gallipoli – John Masefield – William Heinemann – 1917 – p 48

(13) Jutland, An Analysis of the Fighting – John Campbell – Conway Maritime Press – 1986 – p 64

(14) Memoirs of Commander Philip J. Stopford – The Naval Review – http://www.naval-review.org/

The Morning News
The Times

South Façade, St Ouen's Manor (author)

PHILIP'S LETTERS

30/01/1909
Eltham College
Eltham
Kent

My dear Dad

Last Wednesday it froze hard, so that the boys who had skates went skating, but the rest of us went down the field, where there was a small pond, and we made a slide and slid about on it.

You must have been having rather strong winds to blow all those trees down.

One of the drains in the head-master's house was leaking and when it froze it was all covered in ice. I was 4th in the form last week and am 1st this week.

Last Thursday as it was not cold enough to snow, so it rained all night, so that in the morning there was a large swamp on the junior football field and part of it was under water. If it had frozen then we would have had a lot of ice.

It won't be very nice if all the water in Paris freezes, as its people have to be carried about in boats. I saw a picture of someone who had come to Paris being taken to the hotel in a sort of punt, and he had to be hoisted up through a window.

With much love to you all
Your loving son
P.Malet de Carteret

3rd March, 1910
Eltham College
Eltham
Kent

My dear Dad

Thank you very much for the postal order for 2/6. We had the match on Wednesday and we lost by 10 to 5. It was pouring with rain all the time and so it was very hard to run because the ground was so sloshy. I expect why the reason I was so low in English was because my Reproduction marks are always low and Dictation, Reproduction and Reading are all counted as English. For that story competition we are not allowed to write anything that we had read about, or what had happened to us, but it had to be absolutely invented by ourselves. The prize was given by the voting of the class. The boy's who got the prize was called "The Capture of the Steel Pirate"

We had a half? Last Friday for half-term and there is still another to come for one of the boys who has passed his London Matriculation. It will be rather hard for me to keep my place at the top of the form because I only just beat the boy behind me by about 10 marks in the whole of the half term. One boy, who is going up for his Osborne exam has brought back the last time examination paper and when I looked at them everything was fairly easy, except the Latin, which I thought was very hard.

With love to all
Your loving son
P. Malet de Carteret

15th May, 1910
Eltham College
Eltham
Kent

My dear Guy

I wish you a very happy birthday. Have you yet begun Latin, as you said you were going to at the beginning of this term, if so how do you like it? Have you yet seen the comet? I believe it will be visible to the naked eye in a few days. Nothing special has been happening here lately. You might tell Mamie that I was 3rd this week. I found that out this afternoon. How is Kenneth getting on he must have been in bed for over a month on end by now. I hope that you are all quite well

With love from Philip.

Midshipman Philip Reginald Malet de Carteret (1898-1916)

My dear Dad

The sports came off last Tuesday. It was quite a fine day for them. One chap, after winning the quarter mile and half-mile created a record for the college for the mile by doing it in 4 minutes and 51 seconds. As well as having prizes for the first two, or three places as the case may be, the first chap in the race counted for three points, the second two, and the third one. All these points counted towards a Sports Cup, which Drake's (4th term) won, as they got the greatest number of points. Beside the ordinary events, they had two more – a "wheel barrow" and a "sack race". Anyone could go in for these, and you just went in on the spot. I went in for the wheelbarrow race, with another chap who wheeled me. We only got about half-way over the course before the first chaps got in, so we gave up as all the others had done.

After the sports, prizes were distributed by the skipper's wife.

On Wednesday there was a swimming relay race. Each term had 20 competitors who each swam two lengths in the swimming bath and as soon as one finished another started off just like an ordinary relay race. The Drake's won this as well. The Exmouth (sixth term) being second. Our term was last by about half a length, which was not so bad, as last term the first term (so I heard) were three lengths behind.

On Thursday there was the Cross Country Race! It was divided into twp parts – the people over 5 foot 4 inches, and those under. Of course I was an under. The course was all over ploughed fields, through hedges, up most awful hills, and down just as bad ones.

You pretty well had to run all the way. I was absolutely done by the time I came in. In this race there were points for the Cross Country cup just like there were for the Sports cup. The first chap home in the "overs" got 60 points, the second 59 etc. In the unders the first chap got 40 points, the second 39 etc. I did not get a place. The 5th term won this and our term was not last in order but 4th out of 6.

Altogether it was rather a strenuous week, and as everything is now over, we can go to the canteen and get out of training as much as we like, which is always a great thing.

With love from
Your affectionate son Philip.

17th July, 1913
RNC Dartmouth
Devon

My dear Dad

Mumps have fairly broken out here, it has been going on for three or four weeks, but up till last Sunday there were not more than about 10 cases, but now there are from 70 to 80. At one time there was talk of sending us home, but that idea has been given up. I have not yet got it, although the chaps whose beds and chests are all around mine have got it. It has chiefly broken out in the Third term where there are only 30 cadets left. The doctor said it was a good thing to sweat to keep them off, so you see chaps running round and round the gym with three sweaters on, on a hot afternoon, doing their best to sweat as much as possible!

I got my first game of tennis the other day, and found I was most frightfully out of practise – could hardly hit a ball decently, and got double faults every other serve.

We have just reached the few days before the exams when there are no marks. You might think it was rather a slack time, but really it is rather the reverse, as all our spare time is used up in copying in pilotage notes, History notes and Engineering sketches.

Today the Osborne padre and ours swop place, the Osborne one coming here for the day, and ours going off to Osborne.

A new coloured window has been put in the chapel, and it has been dedicated to Captain Scott. Most of the money for it has been got by collections in church.

I have heard that Goddard is coming over to Jersey for the latter part of leave, he has been asking me for information as to how to get back to Dartmouth from there. By the by he won the under 5 foot 4 inches swimming races last Thursday, another chap in our term being second.

With much love from your affectionate son Philip.

1st Feb, 1914
RNC College
Dartmouth
Devon

My dear Dad

How ripping it must have been when the pond was frozen over hard enough for you to stand on. If the frost had continued for a little, I suppose you would have been able to skate. It has been quite the reverse over here. It is quite warm (for February), and sometimes we have a little rain, but never any snow or frost.

I saw in the English papers a few days ago about the extra taxes that were being imposed upon tea and tobacco.

Have the punctures in the motor been mended yet? I suppose it must have rather inconvenienced Grandpa while it was punctured. Did both punctures happen at the same time, and were they in the same wheel or different ones?

Next Saturday is our first whole holiday. We stop work at 11 o'clock in the morning, and then Wynne, Maclean and I are going off to Newton Abbot to watch the usual football match of the College against Blundells school. As a matter of fact, probably Wynne will be playing for the 2nd XV but anyhow Maclean and I will still go and will be able to watch him play.

After the second whole-holiday which comes about thee weeks after the first, the next item on the terms programme is the Entertainment. This comes off on the 7th of March. There is some rumour that Commander Evans is going to give a lecture on the South Polar expedition which he was in, but nobody knows for certain whether the rumour is true or not.

Some balm has been poured into my gaping wound caused by the information that there is going to be a Cross Country race this term, by a rumour which says that only the best dozen or so runners in each term will be chosen to run in the Cross-Country will be chosen by the form they showed in the Sports. I hope to goodness that rumour, at any rate, is true.

Love to all from your affectionate son Philip.

May 16th, 1914
Royal Naval College
Dartmouth
Devon

My dear Guy

Many happy returns of the day. I hope the cartridges were all right – they are of the anchor variety as Vint's have no acorns in stock I hope they will do as well, you can always get them changed I suppose if they don't.

I don't know whether you have heard of the hash I made of things in trying to get to Dartmouth at the beginning of term – I took about 10 wrong trains, and went up and down between Plymouth and Newton Abbot about 20 times, finally arriving at the College at 10.30pm instead of 4 o'clock. We are having quite decent weather here, and one is able to get in a respectable amount of tennis and boating etc. I hope you are having ditto.

I am afraid there is not much news. As no doubt you know most days are the same at college. I got a letter from Ellie the other day which I suppose I had better answer so I will now wind up
Yours etc Philip

My dear Dad
I expect you have guessed the reason why you have not been receiving regular letters – viz : we are not always in harbour. Of course you know that I am not allowed to divulge anything about where we are etc and as a censor examines all letters before leaving the ship, it is not much good trying. I don't need any winter underclothing or suits etc – in fact I am much too hot as it is, besides I would not be able to give you any definite address to send them to.
There is absolutely nothing to tell you without trespassing on forbidden ground so I am afraid all my letters will have to be short.
I am quite well and flourishing and I hope you are the same. How are Ellie and Guy?
I hope Grandpapa is getting better, I am glad to heat that he has made a slight recovery.
With much love to Mamie and you from your affectionate son Philip

p.s Now that I am "snotty", letters should be addressed " P.R. MdeC Esq: R.N."

My dear Dad
Thank you very much for the Postal order which you sent me. We have been rated midshipman and are wearing patches which look most gorgeous.
I have got a telescope from Gieve's and we have all drawn oilskins and sou'westers from the ship's stores so that's all right.
Yesterday afternoon the old Reindeer passed under our stern pitching horribly and carrying a whole lot of troops, I suppose they were a new regiment for Jersey or something. Anyhow I fairly glared at her through my telescope, I think the Tommies were feeling pretty sick – they looked it.
The "snotties" here have been let off keeping watch because we have such a lot of other work to do. I wish I knew where we are going or what we are going to do, but of course I don't know anything about it. Anyhow the Germans seems to be getting rather a rotten time – jolly good job too seeing that they have been getting far too sidey lately. I hope you

and Mamie are quite well and Ellie and Guy. There is nothing more to say, so I had better wind up.

 With much love to all from your affectionate son
 Philip M de Carteret
 Midshipman R.N.

p.s. The Commander of this ship Commander Stopford says that he knew some people out in New Zealand called de Carteret Malet – I wonder if there is any connection.

November 20th

My dear Dad

 Perhaps you would like an account of our late doings, so I will tell you what happened since last you heard of me, which I think was when we were in the Falkland Islands.

 We left the Falkland Islands on October 23rd, and made for the Straits of Magellan which we entered the next day. The next few days we spent in going through the Straits which were very fine. Although the mountains on each side were not very high, the tops of them were covered with snow, and they looked quite like Swiss Mountains. The sea was as calm as anything, and the scenery was for all the world like the Lake of Geneva from Lausanne. Of course it was very cold. I took several photos of both Tierra del Fuego and the American side, but they did not come out very well.

 We got out of the Straits on the evening of the 27th, and proceeded Northwards well out of sight of land.

 We had two store-ships in company which we were escorting. On the night of November 1st we had the action, an account of which you have doubtless by now received from me. It was during this night that we lost touch with our convoy because we increased speed and left them behind.

 The captain spent a long and anxious time until he learnt they had reached port safely and his responsibility was over. As you know, after the action we and the Glasgow proceeded south again. On the evening of November 3rd we entered a channel called Messier Channel which runs parallel to the Chilean coast and joins the Straits of Magellan, East of the ordinary entrance. We had no charts of this channel, but luckily we had an officer on board who had been through it 36 times and practically knew the navigation of it by heart, and he took us through without charts. In some places the channel was no more than 200 yards across. The reason why we used this channel was in case the Germans *got ahead of us and cut us off at the proper entrance to the Straits. However nothing happened, and we reached the Straits on the 5th. We went through the Straits and made for the Falkland Islands which we reached on the 8th. We had orders to proceed to Monte Video, but we simply had to stop at the Falklands for a day to coal. When we had finished we proceeded to Monte Video. But when we were half way there our orders were suddenly cancelled and we were told to return to the Falklands which we reached on the afternoon of the 12th. We have been there ever since. There is one great advantage in staying at one place and that is that we will probably get our mails fairly regularly. I hope everyone at home is quite well. We have got hold of some month old newspapers and are very pleased with life. With much love to all from Philip.*

"The climate of the Falklands has been described by one of the residents as consisting of " nine months winter and three months bad weather" and our experience bore that out. Although it was getting on for midsummer we had several falls of snow and the wind blew with hurricane force at times. A remarkable fact is that few, if any, of the Islanders can swim, as the water is always too cold for bathing. We had a sad example of this during our stay, when a punt containing seven of the volunteer force capsized in crossing a creek in the harbour, and all were drowned. Added to the cold, the amount of kelp that grows in the water takes away most of the chance that even a good swimmer might have." From Commander Stopford's Memoirs(14)

December 26th

My dear Dad

We have left the Falkland Islands at last and have arrived at dear old Abrolhos Rocks again. My hat! But it's hot, being, of course, midsummer. We have not heard anything of the Dresden since the action, and she seems to have escaped altogether although several of our ships are still looking for her. I wonder where our next destination will be, as I am sick of this hole. There are rumours flying around that we are going home, although I do not think this is likely; probably we will go back to Port Stanley again.

Yesterday was Christmas Day. We draped the gunroom with flags and made it look as cheerful as possible and scraped together a plum pudding (tinned) and a few crackers but a Christmas at sea is a very different one from one at home.

Sunday in this ship always seems to be our unlucky day. For instance to-morrow (Sunday) we are going to coal ship, and a pretty hot job it'll be. The "Karlsruhe" is still at large, doing occasional damage to our merchantmen, but we are getting up an organized hunt for her, so I expect she will soon be run to earth.

Hoping you are all well at home, and with much love to all. I remain your loving son – Philip.

Jan 6th 1915

My dear Guy

The mails seem to be going more regularly nowadays, so I seize the opportunity of writing.

There is another rumour going round the ship that we have to be in dock in Devonport by February 19th and so we are going to leave here on the 15th of this month. However, I don't suppose there is any truth in it, – there never is in these rumours.

We have been having a lot of target practice lately with 3 pounder sub-calibre stuck inside the 6" guns, and to-morrow we are going to have a regular battle-practice with the big guns at a target stuck in between two masts of a sunken wreck which is quite close.

We received a mail yesterday. I got a letter which apparently had been stuffed into one of the commander's letters. It contained a set of photos of the family which I had already been sent some time ago. They were very good – did you take them?

There has been no confirmation as yet to the rumour about the Dresden being sunk – I wish to goodness there were.

There is an awful rumour that the "von der Tann" – one of Germany's battle-cruisers has escaped from the North Sea, and is coming down here to slaughter us. I hope, if that is true, that she will at any rate meet the Invincible and the Inflexible, who are homewards bound, before she comes to tackle us, as if not she will wipe us off the face of the earth.

I hope everyone at home is quite well and flourishing.

With much love to all from Philip.

February 15th, 1915

My dear Dad

We are in dock at the present moment, although not in dry dock. We expected to go into dry dock a day or two ago, but another ship bagged our place. We are expecting a store-ship from England here soon – either to-morrow or the day after – and if it comes it ought with luck to bring us some mails, in which case I ought to get a uniform suit which I ordered from Gieve's while we were at the Falkland Islands. There is *also a month's mail's due to us which was sent to Abrolhos after we had left there, and that ought to arrive soon I suppose.*

We are allowed ashore here every afternoon when we are not on duty, but have to be on board again by 7pm.

Last night some French officers came on board from one of the French ships which are here, and were entertained by our officers until very late. They sang songs and had drinks etc, and finished up by chanting the Marseillaise and "It's a long way to Tipperary" several times over and kicking up a most unholy shindig.

There is a Sports Club here which we have been invited to join. You pay your subscription, and you get lawn tennis, racquets, squash and all kinds of other games. It is a great placed. Most of the Gunroom have joined.

There are several snotties here whom we knew at Dartmouth, some even are the same term as we, and we ask some of them to dinner in the Canopus, and in return they ought to (but have not as yet) asked us back. We discuss the numerous actions which we have taken part, and such like interesting subjects.

Allow me with my own lily-white hand to congratulate you on being appointed to the high and mighty post of Jurat! I suppose you spend most of your time now in town attending to the wants of the Island.

I hope everyone at home is quite well and flourishing.

With much love to all. Your affectionate son, Philip.

March 12th, 1915
HMS Canopus

My dear Dad

I received a letter from you yesterday, in which you made three guesses as to what we were going to do after leaving Malta. As you know already the first one was right.

The other night we delivered a night attack on the Dardanelles, the whole ship being pitch dark herself. The mine-sweepers went ahead to sweep for mines of which they picked up several, while we followed on astern, firing at any lights and searchlights which we saw on either shore. Some batteries replied to our fire, but no shells hit us. However it seemed that the Turks did more damage to us than we did to them, for although we only managed to extinguish one or two searchlights, yet they sank two of our mine-sweepers, one I am afraid going down with all hands, the other all were saved.

I believe we are going to start on the bigger forts in a day or two – the Canopus always seems to be in the thick of things. I am enclosing a picture of the Dardanelles taken out of a Daily Paper. It may help to give you some idea of how far we have got up them. If you hear any fatuous rumours about our having advanced 18 miles up the Dardanelles, you may be petty sure they are false, as I don't suppose we are more than 8 to 10 miles up at the very most, but then of course things always do get exaggerated don't they.

The Admiral has called for volunteers of officers (including Gun Room officers) to go in these trawlers and mine-sweepers. All the Gunroom of Canopus has volunteered, but then so many other people have, so I don't suppose we will get much of a chance.

Hoping you are all well at home. With much love to all from Philip.

March 15th, 1915
HMS Canopus

My dear Guy

We spent all last night patrolling about outside the entrance to the Dardanelles, and in the morning, we came across a floating mine.

We opened fire on it with rifles hoping to sink it, but nothing happened, although we hit it heaps of times. Then we tried a maxim, which however was equally ineffective. A 3 pound gun was next tried, and after several shots we at last managed to sink it. That morning we went up the straits a bit, and later on came across another mine, which we sank as before by gun-fire. In the afternoon we went to general quarters, and started firing on some shore batteries which had annoyed us on previous occasions. They returned our fire, and, although the range was very great, they managed to drop some shells pretty close to our Quarterdeck without hitting us however. About 3 o'clock or so we saw three more mines which were all sunk in the same way as the others had been. The reason why so many floating mines were seen about was because every night, the mine sweepers go up to where the mine-field is, and by "creeping" they set free the mines from their moorings, and they float down with the current. About 5.30pm we were relieved of our job by another ship and before leaving for our base, or temporary "home" we pointed out two more mines to her which we had just caught sight of, and left her to sink them. But by this time the forts had woken up, and started to fire on her, hitting her several times.

She returned the fire with great gusto. I hope you are all well at home. Love from Philip.

March 29th, 1915
HMS Canopus

My dear Dad

We have just been to one of the Greek islands round here for a couple of days' stand off.

During the afternoons, the officers were allowed to land, and on the second day I went ashore. The island itself was pretty dull, but there was an Australian camp there with a lot of Australian soldiers in it, and also there were a lot of black troops (Senegalese) who were practising disembarking from a troop-ship. They had all got claw-marks and scars on their faces as if they had been scratched by a panther (of course it was really artificial) but I expect they will give the Turks gyp. We went along the beach, and, as it was rather warm we thought we'd have a bathe, which we did.

The water was very shallow, and we had to wade out for miles before it got deep enough to go under water. It was pretty cold, too, and we were only able to stay in for about 10 minutes. After that we walked about the town (such as it was) and I bought a postcard and a box of Turkish Delight (they call it Greek Delight, as of course they will have nothing to do with Turkey now that war is declared). At 4 o'clock we returned to the ship.

While we were away from our base we heard that a hostile aeroplane had turned up and had dropped two bombs at our aeroplane ship, the first of which went about 100 yards ahead of it and the second only 10 feet away from her side. No damage was done, however, and the aeroplane went away because it was fired on by some anti-aircraft guns.

We are back again at our base, and last night we were patrolling. I don't know when we are going to make our next attack on the forts, but I hope it will be soon. I should have thought it would be fatal to leave them alone for such a long time as we have done, as they have probably mounted more guns all over the place now, but still, I suppose the Admiral knows best. There was some talk of our escorting a damaged ship back to Malta which would have been rather decent especially if we could have got ashore, but that plan has fallen through.

Did you know that Commander Samson the great airman is out here? Anyhow he is, and I expect he will shake things up a bit with his bombs. Thank you for the Gieve waistcoat which turned up a few days ago. It is rather a fine and large contraption, several of the officers here have got them. We call them "funk-waistcoats", and they can scarcely be noticed when worn underneath an ordinary coat. I always stuff mine *on before going into action. Wynne said he owed his life to his "funk-waistcoat" when the Formidable went down.*

With much love to all from
Your affectionate son Philip.

April 4th, 1915
HMS Canopus

My dear Guy

I am sending you a box of Turkish Delight obtained from one of the Greek islands hereabouts. I hope it will reach you safely, and if so that you will like it. I dare say you have heard of Commander Samson the great aviator; well he has sent out for midshipman volunteers to go up in his aeroplane for signalling duties – taking in and sending out Morse Messages. Of course all our gunroom volunteered, and I believe there may be a chance of my going, as I am fairly light and of course the lighter you are the better. I hope so anyhow, as it will be rather fun flying over the Chanak forts and dropping bombs on the 14 inch guns, and seeing them blow up. Of course they will snipe at us, and probably fire shrapnel at us, and we may even have a duel with another aeroplane (there are one or two hostile ones out here) but of course that will all be in the days's work. All one has to do is take in messages probably made by searchlight, and send them out on a little wireless instillation which they have got on most of these aeroplanes. Altogether it ought to be rather fine sport I should think unless we tumble out or get sniped.

The other day we went "Hunning" (as we call it) up the Straits. We came across a few small field guns which opened fire chiefly on the mine-sweepers, but we silenced them without much trouble.

I have not been out mine-sweeping again since that time I wrote about.

Excuse the shortness of this letter, but it is rather doubtful whether I shall catch the mail or not, so there is a bit of a hurry.

With much love to all from Philip.

April 15th, 1915
HMS Canopus at Skyros

My dear Dad

I am very sorry to hear that you have got mumps. I hope by the time you get this letter you will have got over them. Are you isolated from the rest of the family like I was? It always seems to be my fate to write home on coaling days. The last three or four letters have been written just after coaling besides numerous other odd times. Today we are also coaling. I have been having rather a fine time lately. We have just come back from Malta, where however we only stayed for one day to take in stores etc: and then we went to an island called Skyros which we have converted into a base, and we seem to be waiting here indefinitely for transports and things to turn up, as I believe, our captain is in charge of the landing.

We can bathe every day, as of course it is quite warm out here at this time of year. We have been ashore quite often, too, and the other day several of us landed with our rifles, but there is nothing whatsoever to shoot; in fact the island is practically uninhabited except for a few shepherds and some goats which roam about wildly

They don't seem to be getting much forwarder with this Dardanelles show in spite of all the things they say in the papers. The latest aeroplane reports state that they have mounted tons of new guns in places of the old ones which had been destroyed, and the place is practically as impregnable as ever. Still, I suppose these troops ought to shake things up a bit if the landing is successful, especially these black Senegalese troops who have been brought out.

I hope everyone at home is quite well, and that you and Guy have got over your mumps.

With much love to all from
Your affectionate son Philip.

May 2nd, 1915
HMS Canopus

My dear Guy

I wish you many happy returns of the day. Of course this letter will reach you about 3 weeks late, but out here one has to take one's chance of a mail leaving, a thing which never happens unless some steamship or collier has to go to Malta for supplies in which case she takes the fleet's mails with her.

I suppose I may as well tell you about the lucky accident which resulted in my getting a slight scratch which I proudly call a "wound". I was sitting in my boat which was alongside the pontoon on the beach waiting for the wounded to come along. Shrapnel was bursting overhead, and the bullets were splashing all around us, several in fact, got into the boat. I was hit on the head by a shrapnel bullet and started bleeding like a pig. Luckily the thing was spent, and so, after being bandaged up at a field ambulance place, I was quite all right. The firing was very heavy that day, and bullets were dropping all around us. I picked up a couple as souvenirs. Besides all that, a Turkish warship anchored up the straits, suddenly opened fire across the Gallipoli peninsular, at the British transports and men-of-war. However, no harm was done. Since then, every morning at about 4 a.m. that ship has fired about 10 rounds at the British fleet concentrated off Gaba Tepe without doing any damage. After letting this go on for a day or two, passively, we thought we would give her a little surprise, so one fine morning an hour before their normal show began (viz 3 a.m.) every battleship, at a given signal, loosed off a couple of 12 inch guns at her, while a seaplane went up to see what the effect was. The latter reported that our salvo went about 100 yards short and had had the effect of clearing the ship out. She reappeared again however and since then, almost every morning at about 3.30 a.m. we exchange the compliments of the season with her. She has registered a hit on a collier (nothing serious) and several shots have pitched quite close to the Canopus, fragments of the shells falling on the Quarterdeck. A Hun aeroplane has also started to make itself objectionable, and has turned up here, and this morning started dropping bombs at a sort of captive balloon affair which we keep from which to observe how the land fighting goes on. The animals (meaning the captive balloon) escaped being bombed, and the Hun aeroplane got well peppered with shrapnel for its pains and cleared out.

The Admiral here seems rather a wag. Anyhow he is rather fond of surprise packets for the unsuspecting Turks at a given signal from him. The other day he gave the order that at 7 p.m. that day all ships were to open fire with shrapnel (concentrating on a certain square of land where the Turkish trenches were) and fired rapid salvoes for ¼ of an hour when every ship would cease fire. Accordingly we did this, and, at a given signal we all opened fire together and gave the Turks one of the warmest ¼ of an hours they have ever had. I should think that every ship (warship) there must have got rid of 75 to 100 rounds of 6 inch shrapnel in those momentous 15 minutes.

You ought to be out here if you are feeling at all dull – I can assure you there is no lack of excitement in this part of the world. Of course I have given up all hopes of aeroplaning.

I see a good deal of de Wett here – I suppose you know he is in the London which is out here. He is quite well and flourishing.

I hope everyone at home is quite well. With love to all – hope I shall be home soon from Philip. p.s. We have been coaling to-day again.

May 6th, 1915
HMS Canopus

My dear Dad

I am sending you two photographs. They are not up to much, I know. One is of the Canopus (the thing in the foreground is an oar) taken by me, and the other is of her Commander (P.J. Stopford R.N.) not taken by me. There has been rather a fuss made about photos lately as it turns out that someone has been sending films containing pictures valuable to the enemy to Malta to be developed, and the photographers there have let some percolate through to Italy, so nowadays one has to obtain permission to send any photos at all out of the ship.

All the Canopus' snotties except two (myself being one) are being borne temporarily in the "London" where they are employed in conveying the wounded men in boats from the shore to various transports which are acting as hospital ships. I am glad I am not one of them as it appears that they get practically no food on board the "London", besides that there are 29 people in the Gunroom, which means an unholy squash, and they have to sling their own hammocks, whereas if they want clean clothes they have to wash their own dirty ones themselves. Altogether they do not get much of a time, the only advantage being that they can pick up as many shells etc: as curios off the beach as they like, but as I have already got a Turkish bayonet and several rifle and shrapnel bullets, that does not worry me any. The other day 4 of them managed to get off to this ship for a few hours and they seemed very sorry for themselves.

A few days ago we were treated to rather an interesting spectacle. The Admiral had sent us to see about an observation hut of which he suspected the existence round the corner, and he sent us to wipe it out. We went along there and landed some troops from a destroyer who found a trench containing 26 Turks all fast asleep. Our fellows charged the trench, woke the Turks up rather suddenly with cold steel, killing 8, capturing 16 of which 3 were wounded and 2 escaped without a single casualty on our side. They then demolished the observation hut and returned to the destroyer. The whole thing took place not very far inland so we could watch it quite comfortably from the ship through our telescopes.

George (as we call the Turkish ship which I mentioned in my last letter to Guy) has not been doing much in the matinee line lately. Yesterday he fired two ineffectual shots, but before that and since then he has been remarkably quiet. I expect he had been thoroughly cowed.

We seem to be getting on as well as is to be expected on land though not much news is given to us as to what results are being obtained.

There has been rather an absence of mails lately, the last lot we received being a good fortnight ago, but of course we think nothing of that having been without them for two months or so at the beginning of the commission.

I hope you are quite well and are bearing up bravely under the strain of being a Jurat.

With much love to all from your affectionate son, Philip.

June 11th, 1915
HMS Canopus at Malta

My dear Guy

We arrived in Malta all right without being torpedoed, and will probably stay here at least 10 days to have several minor repairs done, so we ought to have a fairly decent time of it.

It is simply appalling the amount of French ships there are in the harbour compared with the number of English ones. There are at present a dozen large French battleships and cruisers beside several Destroyers and Torpedo boats as against 3 English battleships and about 2 cruisers. As for our Torpedo craft: they are all out looking for submarines and only come in for a day at a time to coal and provision. The French navy seem to be doing absolutely nothing.

An Enemy submarine was yesterday reported to be hiding in one of the bays around Malta, and also a supply ship of ours was reported torpedoed just outside Lemnos and several other rumours have been flying around like that lately, but nothing has ever come of them.

I went on leave yesterday for the afternoon and hope to do so a good many times yet before we leave – I have reckoned it out that with luck I can get ashore 3 afternoons out of 5 which is not bad going, although there is of course a good deal to do on the two days you are aboard. There is a topping bathing place just outside the town, and of course at this time of year the water is ripping and warm. The Albion is here with us, and Maclean is in her: I am going out with him this afternoon – I believe he is going to get himself tattooed, and it will be rather fun to watch him in his agony, especially if he gets blood-poisoning or something. A good many of Canopus' gunroom have got themselves tattooed on the arm, I have not got as far as that yet.

After we have finished with Malta most people think we are going back again to the Dardanelles. Some optimists go so far as to say that we are going home, but I don't believe that. I have given up expecting to come home ages ago after the disappointments we have had. In fact I shall not believe we are going home until either I see the official orders or am told personally by the captain, that we are going to Devonport.

I hope you will excuse the shortness of this letter, but there is no news to tell you, and being in Malta there are of course no submarines, mines, forts, Torpedo boats, shells, battleships, aeroplanes or such like things to annoy us. I hope you are quite well – I suppose you are in the middle of the summer term.

With much love from Philip.

June 19th, 1915
HMS Canopus at Malta

My dear Dad

Am sending you the key of my sea-chest in case you have not been able to open it. Towards the bottom of it you will find heaps of books. Out of these please select "Inman's Nautical Tables! and "Halls Navigation", and send them to me. We have started instructions again having knocked off while at the Dardanelles, and our Navigating Officer has refused to teach us Navigation unless we each have these books and has ordered us to send home for them at once which I hereby have done.

It appears that we have been ordered to remain in Malta until at least the end of the month to have some repairs done in the engine room. We are taking the opportunity therefore of having several other minor repairs done in other parts of the ship, and although we have not actually gone into dry-dock, yet the ship is crowded with dockyard hands, and the hammering and riveting goes on practically day and night. Unfortunately they are mending the hole in the Quarterdeck amongst other things, and so now it will be no longer noticeable, and we will present a much more pacified and less warlike appearance to visitors, but I expect that will soon be remedied after another month or so at the Dardanelles. We are getting as much leave as possible, although now that we are doing instructions in addition to our ordinary work it does not amount to very much, and we are living on the accumulated surplus of our pay. We had hoped at one time that the Commander might give us snotties 48 hours leave if we stayed long enough in Malta, but have long since given up all idea of that.

The "Albion" sailed this morning – presumably for the Dardanelles – with both Maclean and Bev de Jersey on board.

While in Malta we are taking the chance of replenishing and adding to our store of gramophone records – we have got rather a decent gramophone which belongs to the Gunroom Mess – for of course having heard the same old records for months on end without a change, they are apt to get a bit stale, besides several having been broken in the crash of cannonades and the furious strife!

The walls of the Gunroom, although bare of woodwork which was stripped down ages ago when we had a fire-scare in the South Atlantic, are now ornamented with Turkish rifles, bayonets, entrenching tools and shells arranged in fantastic positions all over the place and they look very imposing and warlike.

I never asked permission to send that last set of photos which I sent home, as I clean forgot all about it, But I don't suppose any fuss will be made about them, in fact I doubt if they will even censor the letter, and anyhow the photos are so rotten as to be absolutely useless to a Hun.

With much love to all from your affectionate son, Philip.

> June 23rd, 1915
> HMS Canopus at Malta

My dear Guy

I am sending you a few postcards, and hope that they are the kind you want. There are not so many of the kind to be had in Malta, but what there are I hope are not duplicates of what you have already got. One of them you will notice is an imaginary picture of the battle of the Falklands Islands.

We are still at Malta and having a good time. Last Monday I went out for a sail with another chap in a little sailing boat which we hired. There was a strong breeze, and we went outside the harbour and tacked up against the wind for about 5 or 6 miles. It was pretty rough in the open, but we turned into a little sheltered cove where we anchored and bathed. We stayed there for some time, and then came back to Valetta at a terrific pace with the wind directly astern of us.

They have almost finished mending the hole in our Quarterdeck, and now I don't suppose we will stay here much more than a week so we must make the best of our time here.

This morning we were to have shifted our billet and gone alongside another wharf further up the harbour, but somehow it didn't come off.

Our captain has started a scheme in which about 60 of the ships company together with 6 officers (2 Lieutenants and 4 snotties) go to a place about ¾ of a mile away and do rifle and squad drill at 6.15 every morning for exercise. It starts to-morrow morning. I shall be going the day after to-morrow I suppose. It is rather a bore because it stops one having a bathe before breakfast, and rifle and squad drill at the best of times is horrible.

With much love from Philip.

July 3rd, 1916
HMS Canopus at Mudros

My dear Dad

I was very sorry to hear that you were having trouble with your teeth. I hope you have got over it by now without the loss of too many of them.

We left Malta, as we expected, the day after I wrote my last letter, and arrived at Mudros two days later without meeting any submarines or anything more warlike than a French hospital ship on the way. We are now stuck in the harbour, and likely to stay there for an indefinite time so far as I can see. It appears now that the reason why we stayed so long in Malta was because they were trying to decide at the Admiralty whether to send the Canopus home or to send her out here again. They eventually decided on the latter, chiefly because one of the other ships of our class out here has developed serious boiler troubles, and they have been forced to pay her off, and of course they could not spare two ships from the Dardanelles at so short an interval, and so back we had to go again and here we are. Still it was rather a pity – so near and yet so far sort of touch.

You must know we are the crack ship out here both as regards efficiency and having been out here so long. We know all the routine so to speak. All the skippers of trawlers swear by us, and say that they will never go mine-sweeping up the Straits unless the Canopus is there to back them up, as they say that all the other battle-ships seem frightened of letting off a round or two at the Turkish batteries, and the result is the trawlers get thoroughly shelled.

We on the other hand are rather prodigal than otherwise with our ammunition, in fact once or twice our captain has been told about it by the Admiral. But of course that was in the high and far-off times, and nowadays our guns are drooping and wilting like flowers for want of a shot through them.

Thank goodness at any rate we are in a fairly decent billet in the harbour – that is to say near the entrance. That means the water is fairly clean and consequently we are able to bathe over the side which we were not allowed to do last time we were here when we were further up the harbour, and the water was filthy.

They seem to be getting on very well at Seddul Bahr and V beach according to the reports, although we are remaining stationary at Gaba Tepe. This of course we are doing on purpose as we don't wish to advance there, and the Turks can't budge us out of our position as we are so well entrenched.

The submarines which created such a scare a few weeks ago now seem to have evaporated into thin air for which I am profoundly thankful and hope they will never make their appearances again. Rumour – always to the fore- has it that there are 5 Hun submarines up at Chanak which are unable to get down because of a net which we have stretched across the Straits; but I think that is rather a fatuous yarn.

With much love to all from your affectionate son Philip.

July 13th, 1915
HMS Canopus at Meteline

My dear Dad

Thank you very much for the Quid which you sent me. You ask when I was rated Midshipman. In the last Navy List the date was August 4th, 1914, and certainly I receive midshipman's pay – 1/9d a day – from that date.

We are at present lying in a place called Port Iero in the island of Meteline (pronounced Mettyleeny) off the coast of Smyrna. We are on the Smyrna Patrol, i.e. in charge of the operations out here. It is not a bad place as Greek places go – you can get good sailing as there is always a wind. The Gunroom have clubbed together to hire a native sailing-boat for a week with a man to look after her. She lies alongside the ship all day, and whenever we want to go for a picnic or anything, why we take our own boat. It is much more satisfactory than having to rely on the Commander letting us have one of the ship's boats which he would be very unlikely to do, as there is a lot of boat-work to do and they would all be required for duties.

One can always get good bathing too, both from the ship's side and from the shore which is a great thing. The water is always warm here, so one can bathe even in a gale of wind. By dint of much practising chiefly carried out at a ripping bathing place in Malta, I can dive off the Quarterdeck. I think we are pretty well a fixture here, although of course one can never tell – we thought we were a fixture at the Abrolhos Rocks and again at the Falkland Islands.

The snotty whom I told you about who missed the ship when he went to Malta has now made up for his bad luck through the captain's decency who has sent him to Malta for a fortnight by the first ship that left for there from Mudros; he is there now I suppose – the lucky blighter. Still, I suppose he deserves it.

I had not heard anything about de Wet's accident on a pony at Malta until I got the family's lurid tidings yesterday – I suppose he will be all right again by now, I hope so anyway.

One of our snotties applied to be sent to one of the trawlers out here engaged in patrol and despatch work – and got it too. She is one of the latest type of trawlers and mounts a 3 pounder gun and is fitted with wireless. He will be 2nd in command, the captain being a Lieutenant R.N. I should think it would be all right, but only for a short time as you would soon get sick of it. He does not seem particularly enthusiastic about the post though he says he likes it well enough.

We coaled this morning from a collier which had been with us at Gaba Tepe during the early days of the proceedings there. She was the one (I don't remember whether I told you about her but I think I did) who got struck by a large Turkish shell during one of the old "morning hates" Although she has been repaired at Malta there are still a few splinter holes left in her ventilating cowls and funnel. She is quite an old friend therefore.

I hope your teeth and gums are not giving you any more trouble – toothache is a rotten show altogether isn't it?

With much love to all from your affectionate son Philip.

August 3rd, 1915
HMS Canopus, Metylene

My dear Dad

Some time ago I ordered 2 suits of white duck from Gieve's besides a few collars and cap-covers, which I was rather in need of. They have just arrived here, so I am just wondering about the inevitable bill (unless it has already come) – so I hope that will be all right.

The Gunroom is at present very empty of inhabitants. Our full strength used to be 1 sub, 1 clerk, 1 snotty R.N.R. and 10 snotties – 13 all told. Since then 2 have gone sick, 2 are in trawlers, 2 are going to H.M.S. "Doris", 1 has left for home (being too delicate or something to stand the strain) and 1 is on leave in Malta. Thus we are reduced to 5 all told.

It is exactly a year since I joined the Canopus – a bit more as a matter of fact because we joined on the Monday night and it is now Tuesday afternoon. Although it seems as if we had been in the ship a long time, yet it doesn't seem as long as a year to me. Anyhow we have managed to cram a good deal of excitement into that one year. I wonder when we shall next sight Devonport – the first step towards home.

An extraordinary looking destroyer came into port this morning. She had enormously tall masts and several queerly place guns which turned out to be 4 inch. We discovered eventually that she was a destroyer which we had been building for the Portuguese Navy, but which, on completion, we had bought from her.

We are expecting a mail some time this evening, at about 6 p.m., we generally get one regularly once a week, every Tuesday, which is not so bad. I hope there will be something for me.

We are still lying at anchor in Port Iero without much prospect of anything turning up. It is appallingly hot, but unfortunately the water round the ships is so dirty that it is impossible to get a decent bathe from the ship's side, but you have to go away from the ship in a small boat.

Nothing further seems to have been heard about submarines, but I expect there is at least one outside the harbour, waiting for all that.

There is absolutely no news to tell you – we simply exist on as best we can.

I hope everyone is quite well. With love from your son Philip.

August 1915
HMS Rattlesnake, Port Iero

My dear Dad

I have been sent to the destroyer Rattlesnake for a short time (about a fortnight I expect) to learn Navigation etc. We are engaged in Patrol work off the Smyrna coast and it is great sport. This morning we returned from a 3 day patrol having done nothing particularly thrilling although we stopped and boarded nearly every vessel and steamer we saw. You see our job is to blockade Smyrna and the surrounding coast and to prevent any contraband of war pass. As a matter of fact one of the smaller ships we stopped had a ton of wheat (which is contraband on board) but as her papers were correct we let her go. We now put in 3 days in Port Iero before going on patrol for another 3 days. It is not worth while addressing your letters to HMS Rattlesnake as we are in port every 3 days, and I can easily go across to the Canopus to collect my mail.

You went across to Guernsey in a destroyer once didn't you? But still there is no harm in describing the Rattlesnake.

She is a fairly modern craft with a compliment of about 95 men and 5 officers, mounts 1 4 inch gun and 3 pounder and several 18" Torpedo tubes. She has a speed of 27 knots. Of course the Officers quarters were rather crowded seeing there was an officer on board for taking charge of the prize crew if we took a prize besides yours humbly, but I sleep on a couch in the Ward Room and shared the First Lieutenant's cabin for washing purposes and so am quite comfortable. At sea I keep 3 hours watch a day and the remainder of the time I take sights, fix the ship's position twice daily, find the error of the compass and generally mess about picking up Navigation.

We carry 5 officers as I said before. One Lieutenant Commander (the captain) 1 Lieutenant (the 1st Lieutenant) 1 sub, 1 gunner and 1 Engineer officer. They are all very decent especially the 1st Lieutenant and the sub. I don't know what work I will do in harbour as it has not yet been settled (we only arrived this morning) but I expect it will consist of correcting charts and bringing the Sailing Directory and Light Lists up to date. Altogether I am having a topping time and hope I stay here till the end of the war. At present we have just finished coaling and most of the ship's company have gone ashore.

By the bye I made a mistake in my last letter in saying that the Torgat Reis had been sunk by a British submarine in the Sea of Marmora. Apparently the signal read "One of the Torgat Reis class" namely Barbarossa. Still it doesn't much matter which one it was though it would be decent to think that our former "hate" would hate us no more – I expect she soon will be sunk with any luck sooner or later.

I believe our troops are getting on splendidly in the Gallipoli Peninsular and advancing fast. We are of course leading a very passive existence compared with when the troops first landed at Gaba Tepe.

I only wish the Rattlesnake was covering the Australian's Left Flank as she was a couple of months ago – then we'd see some sport. Seeing that the official censor is out of the ship, I am going to censor this letter myself, and stamp it as such.

With much love to you all from your affectionate son,
Philip

September 5th, 1915
HMS Canopus, Port Iero

My dear Dad

My time in the Rattlesnake is up now and I have returned to the Canopus much to my disgust. The reason for that was the new Commander (the old one having left) thought it was not advisable to have so many midshipmen out of the ship, in trawlers and destroyers at once but that we ought to be all in the Canopus so that we could be given regular courses of instruction. Accordingly he has recalled us all and now we have a fixed routine altogether. We go for a route march at 5.30 every morning, and the rest of the day is used up with instructions, physical drills, signal exercises etc: etc: He also shakes the ship's company up a good deal and has totally revised the stations for coaling ship. The consequence was that this morning we took in 400 tons in slightly under 2½ hours, an average of about 165 tons an hour and our record.

Another item of news is that our sub (A.E. B. Giles) has received the D.S.O. He got it quite suddenly a day or two ago. Apparently during the Falkland Islands action (He was in the Inflexible) he went down below and closed some Water-Tight doors or something of the sort thus saving the ship from sinking or at any rate being disabled. Nobody quite knows what he did and he refuses to tell anyone about it and gets quite shy and bashful if you mention anything about it and positively bored if anyone congratulates him. Still it is a great achievement, though it was funny him not hearing of it till now.

Not until the 15th of this month does our time as midshipman properly start. All the time before this had it been peace time would have been spent at Dartmouth, in the training cruiser or on leave. I don't suppose the extra time we have put in will make any difference to our seniority, but we will take our time with the others starting from Sept 15th.

Mammy and Guy seem to be having a very pleasant time in London in spite of it being War Time, and they do not seem to find it so changed as one might expect. I only hope to goodness the Zeppelins keep clear of London while they are there.

All kinds of rumours have been reaching us as to England being so hard up for men on the continent that they are not going to send out any more troops go Gallipoli, also that the Italians are going to send an Expeditionary Force to the Dardanelles and Bulgaria has joined in against us.

I wish one could get some reliable information out here without having to wait for the English papers, also that the Press Messages were more definite and truthful.

There was a concert on board the Canopus a night or two ago got up amongst ourselves, but I was in the Rattlesnake at the time and so did not see it, but I was told that it was a great success. The captain afterwards got up and said he expected the Canopus would stay here the whole of the winter.

I believe our old sub (Flynn) who left us to go to a destroyer is coming back again so that we will have 2 subs though of course it is not quite certain.

Hoping that you are all quite well and love from
Your affectionate son, Philip.

September 14th, 1915
HMS Canopus

My dear Guy

You must have had a ripping time of it in London (or are you still there?) Of course it is ages since you were there last but I should think that would make it all the more interesting to go there after such a long time and having forgotten most of the things there.

I was very pleased to receive a photograph of Mammy and you this afternoon, although I did not think it was a very good likeness seeing that you looked as if you had just received news that all your living relatives had kicked the bucket not to mention the Germans having won the war.

Last Sunday being of course a free day more or less we got the Commander's permission to use one of the boats, and after dinner the whole gunroom set off on a picnic taking our tea with us. We sailed across the harbour to a place which we call Naboth's vineyard because it is full up with the most delicious grapes.

As soon as we got there, all the Greeks fussed round and insisted on supplying us with a huge basket of the most luscious grapes (which of course we accept with great vim giving him a tin of biscuits, some sardines and condensed milk in exchange at which he seemed mightily pleased).

We bathed before tea and then boiled our own water on an open-air fire and sat down to a sumptuous feed on the grub which we brought with us and which proved ample. After tea we slacked about generally, some going for walks and others stopping behind. By this time the wind had dropped completely and there was a flat calm. Luckily for us however at about 5.30 a breeze sprang up and we were able to sail back to the ship instead of having to pull back which we should otherwise have had to do.

I am writing this letter under very trying circumstances as Flynn (the sub) insists on my playing the gramophone at the same time, so I have to sort of jam on a record and write a few lines while it is playing and trust to luck to remembering where I left off in the letter. Also I have to catch the post before turning in seeing the mail leaves at some unearthly hour to-morrow morning (about 4 a.m.)

This afternoon I received my second dose of inoculation and am now finished with the "body-snatchers" (doctors). One good result of this inoculation is that they let one off the route-march at 5.30 a.m. to-morrow morning because it is supposed to be bad to take exercise immediately after the operation.

For some obscure and mysterious reason the Commander has decreed that no snotties shall bathe before breakfast. Of course we are all frightfully sick at this as the early morning is about the best time to have a dip although the water is pretty filthy, but anyhow we can always get into the ditch in the dog-watches after a strenuous game of deck-hockey which we almost invariably play; the War droom joining in with the Gun room and playing together.

At present we have got two subs in the mess (Flynn having arrived this morning) but I think the other one (Giles) is soon leaving; anyhow he has applied to go in a destroyer.

Love to all from Philip

October 3rd, 1915
HMS Canopus , Port Iero

My dear Dad

I hope the Loan Exhibition came off well and plenty of good was forthcoming. The photos are all old ones and very badly taken but as I happened to be in a photographic mood I printed them for something to do and hereby enclose a few copies some of which I have already sent home.

Both our Wardroom and Gunroom have got up a racing Galley's crew. We go out rowing in the captain's galley every morning and some times in the evening as well. The idea is to eventually take on a rival crew of the Euryalus (our fellow sufferer at Port Iero of the same class as the Aboukir, Cressy and Hogue). But seeing that the Euryalus cannot raise more than 5 snotties altogether and a galley's crew consists of 7 hands (6 and a coxswain) I doubt very much whether our race at any rate will come off. Still we practice very assiduously under the padre's coaching.

The Euryalus by-the-bye has been at Port Iero even longer than we have so I should think she must be pretty well fed up with it. If you remember, she played a very minor part in the Battle of the Bight at the beginning of the war when Rear Admiral Christian flew his flag there.

We are engaged in making numerous preparations for the winter, so it looks as if we were going to stay here for months yet. For instance all the flimsy wooden piers and landing stages used by the Greeks are being replaced by respectable concrete ones built at the expense of the admiralty and guaranteed to stand the winter gales. Also another very good thing which is being done is that a make-shift hockey ground is being made ashore:

Where, with any luck we should be able to have some good amusement later on, they have only just found a suitable place and have not yet actually started levelling it off roughly so I don't know whether the enterprise will be a success or not.

The weather has suddenly taken a remarkable turn for the better, so although last week we were in full blues, now we are in ducks again and bathing daily. I only hope it lasts.

The other day the Euryalus went out for a few days to take General Hamilton across to Salonika, but she is back again up this morning. Goodness knows what Sir Ian Hamilton wants to go to Salonika for, but still he went there, and I saw the fact mentioned in the press telegram. Where on earth did you see that report about a German submarine being caught just off Metylene? I assure you it is quite a fictitious rumour since no submarine has been caught anywhere near here although one has been seen several times. I expect the report got into some papers through Athens which is almost as unreliable as the Berlin fabrications. I only wish to goodness a submarine could be caught out here as goodness knows they have done enough damage; although not lately, I saw the Rattlesnake mentioned in Admiral de Roebeck's despatches the other day for good work in sweeping up the Straits.

With much love from your affectionate son Philip.

October 11th, 1915
HMS Canopus, Port Mudros

My dear Guy

I hope the family has received a mail or two lately from me because I hear that it is quite possible that the collier Craigstone which took one of our mails from Port Iero to Malta has been sunk by a German submarine on its way there. This however is not at all certain but only rumour but anyhow I thought it would do no harm to scribe another epistle.

The Olympic went out of harbour this morning at about 7.30; not however before we had pulled once round her in the galley to examine her at close quarters. My word she is colossal! She dwarfs every other ship in the harbour, and the wash which she kicked up with her screws as she was turning round would have swamped a small boat.

There are all sorts and kinds of ships in the harbour – how I wish I had my camera! French ships of every description, English transport and liners, battleships from the Lord Nelson class down to the ancient Mars, cruisers ancient and modern, monitors with 14" guns and tripod masts, smaller monitors with 9.2 s and 6" guns, some of the latest destroyers of the L class, submarines, hospital ships, colliers, store-ships, mine-sweepers, mine-layers, trawlers, torpedo boats etc,etc, etc. almost every *kind of ship that was ever built has a representative in Mudros harbour, and all are under Admiral Wemyss. Of course it is impossible to bathe since the whole harbour is covered with ships refuse, soapy water, old tins and boxes etc and all floating about promiscuously, and the stink which rises from it is the distinctive smell of Mudros harbour.*

War with Bulgaria is I believe very imminent. Some Bulgarian guns are said to have fired a few shots the other day at our trawlers and destroyers patrolling the Bulgarian coast near Dediogatch in the Gulf of Xeros, and the Russian trawlers are also supposed to have been engaged, Certain ships have already been told off to deal with the town of Dediogatch in case of war; they have got their orders cut and dried so that immediately war is declared they can carry on.

There are rumours also that Greece is not as friendly towards us as she might be. Goodness knows what will happen if we go to war with her which personally I think is not likely to happen. We shall at any rate bag all their islands like Lemnos, Imbros, Tenedos and Metylene etc which would be quite worth having; also it would be rather fun to bombard Salonika and Athens and a few more of their towns near the coast.

I wonder whether we shall go to Suvla Bay. It is rather a fine place I hear. At any rate there is plenty of excitement for you get fired at the whole time – much worse than Gaba Tepe which is now from all accounts quite harmless. Of course it is quite possible that we shall go back to Iero again as soon as our captain is well, but I hope we go to Suvla or do some bombarding on the Bulgarian Coast.

Hope you are quite well. Chin-chins to all from Philip.

October 19th, 1915
HMS Canopus, Suvla Bay

My dear Grandmamma

Thank you so much for the quid which you sent me. As you know we are at Suvla at present which is the place where the latest landing took place. It is quite a different place from Gaba Tepe, as it is much flatter and there are no steep cliffs but only a gentle slope leading up to the top of a cliff about a mile away from the beach. Our trenches are about 1½ miles inland.

Apparently there was not anything like so much opposition to this landing as there had been to the other ones; in fact if it had not been for misunderstood orders or something our troops could have pushed on much further inland before entrenching themselves. But then there is always some bungle or other somewhere on these occasions. It seems to be a very half-hearted show here altogether. True the ships fire a few rounds every day, but the Turks scarcely ever seem to reply to our fire and even when they do they don't seem to do much damage. As a matter of fact during the last two or three days or so they have bucked up considerably, I think it must be because they have received their fortnightly (or whatever it may be) supply of ammunition. Anyhow last Sunday they blazed off in fine style, first at a store-ship or two lying inside the net and which they only missed by a few feet, then they had a go at our artillery ashore and succeeded in knocking out a 60 pounder field gun, they then started shelling the beaches with a result of several dead mules. Altogether it was quite a "hate" for them.

They don't seem to pay much attention to us battleships, and although the "Glory" (our fellow comrade out here) has been struck three times (before we appeared) yet up to date we are scratch less although shells meant for the unprotected transports etc: beyond us frequently go whistling over our heads.

The greatest pest here are the flies. They simply swarm. Of course they all come from the shore, being blown on board by the winds. I should have thought that in the middle of October it would have been too cold for them to live, but they apparently seem to flourish, although the cold has made them very sluggish so that instead of settling on your face for an instant like any self-respecting fly and flying away again, they stay there for simply ages – until they are driven off in fact. Still that same sluggishness makes them all easier to "swat". In time I suspect they will all die like cockroaches have of which we have also as a pest.

The wounded here amount to about 100 a day, of which only from 20 to 30 are casualties by gun-fire etc; the remainder being all dysentery cases, a disease which has been raging through the whole of the Gallipoli peninsular for months past. A short time in Malta, however soon sets then right.

I wonder whether they will ever wind up this show out here or whether it will drag on until the European War is over – it certainly looks like it at present.

I hope you are all well at Bon air.

Love to all from your affectionate son (!) Philip

Grandma was Elizabeth (nee Poingdestre) who was born 16th November, 1841 and died aged 95 on 8th January, 1937 in her rooms at Plaisance, St Lawrence.

She was an heiress from a wealthy family and her inheritance funded the restoration of St Ouen's Manor at the turn of the 20th century.

Nov 3rd, 1915
HMS Canopus, Mudros

My dear Dad

We left Suvla on Saturday night at about midnight and arrived at Mudros early on Sunday morning. Everybody was certain that we were going to be torpedoed and as we ought to have been by rights, considering the clock work regularity with which a battleship leaves the net at Suvla once a week at night. In fact whenever the Turks see three battleships together in Suvla Bay they know for certain that one of them will leave that night between 10 p.m. and midnight so all they have got to do is station a submarine just outside the net and they are sure to get a bag. One of us is sure to be copped sooner or later unless they alter the routine. However we managed to escape them this time but to wake up for it, when about an hour's time from our destination the fog which up till then had been fairly thick suddenly lifted for an instant and disclosed to the horrified officers on the bridge the bleak coast of Lemnos not ¼ of as mile ahead. We were moving along at 13 knots at the time too. A warning cry from the look-out – Breakers right ahead! Both engines went full speed astern together, and we came to a dead stop about 400 yards from the shore luckily in deep water. A current must have set us off course and of course the fog made navigation very difficult as we dared not go too slow for fear of submarines. However we proceeded on our way nothing daunted and arrived in Mudros at about 7 a.m. quite safely. That day we had a bit of a slack time and received a fairly large mail as we had not had one for a good fortnight, also an outfitter from Gieve's who has taken up his abode here came on board. I was forced to order another blue uniform as I have only got one which I wear everyday and which is getting decidedly shabby. He took my measurements and despatched the order to Gieve's which included a couple of shirts and ½ a dozen socks which are not procurable out here. Things like boots etc: can be got on board.

Next day – November 1st – (I don't think I shall forget that date as long as I live, the anniversary of the sinking of the Good Hope and the Monmouth) we celebrated it by taking in ammunition to replenish the stock we had fired away at Suvla. After ammunitioning ship we prepared for provisioning ship. The store ship did not come alongside till next day (yesterday) and we spent the morning filling up with provisions and stores

Nov 26th, 1915
HMS Canopus, Mudros

My dear Guy

Congratulations on passing the Cambridge Junior exam and

receiving such a high class-certificate. I got your letter of Nov 18th and also the one containing the two photos of the family at its ease in the tent in front of the chapel which I thought were very good- thanks awfully for them. What miserable luck on the chap who got shot in the face by his pal whom you were telling me about. I should think his people must be pretty sick about it especially as he was their one and only.

I suppose we shall coal ship to-morrow; there are 900 tons to come in which will take a goodish time unless we do an extra record coaling. We were to have provisioned ship to-day but somehow or other the store-ship never turned up so we will have to leave that for another day. When we are complete with all the necessaries of life we will wend our slow way to Port Iero there to lie in stagnation till the end of the war while our own sides become chocked with clusters of barnacles and sea-weed. Three months at Port Iero, like Albrolhos Rocks gives one some faint idea of what German sailors must be feeling like after 16 months of decay in the Kiel Canal. Certainly I don't envy them.

Judging from the state of the wind and sea in Mudros Harbour at present I should say they were having a rare old South Westerly gale at Suvla Bay. Thank goodness we are not there as we had quite enough trouble last time besides losing a picket boat and a steam pinnace. I rather doubt if they will be able to hold on to the Suvla position all through the winter as it is so exposed both by land and sea. Of course ever since Lord Kitchener was out here (you remember he came out here the other day) there have been the most astonishing rumours flying around as to what he is supposed to have said. Suvla Bay is to be evacuated or the troops there at any rate to retire to Anzac, a new landing to be effected shortly, 300,000 more troops coming out here etc:etc:etc: You know how these rumours start. – someone overhears someone else telling a third person who got it direct from so-and-so who is Kitchener's valet.

After that last bust-up when the Prince George put into Kephals to avoid a submarine, these craft seem rather to have obliterated themselves at any rate in these waters though I still believe they are still pretty active in the Doro Channel which is the shortest route from Malta to Salonika and where they hope to torpedo a few of our transports or store ships. Of course for that very reason the Doro Channel is studiously avoided by our ships and the wily Hun submarine has perforce to go hungry or at any rate to content himself with a few small unimportant craft.

Hope you are quite fit and well
Love to all from Philip.

Midshipman Philip Reginald Malet de Carteret (1898-1916)

Nov 26th, 1915
HMS Canopus, Mudros

My dear Dad

Many thanks for that ripping warm muffler which you knitted for me. It was just the thing I wanted for some enterprising person had "lifted" my one and only remaining one with the result that I would have gone muffler-less during the middle watch last night if I hadn't borrowed some one else's for the occasion. This morning your gift arrived. We had a topping big mail this morning. I think the idea of a mail having been sunk is rather far-fetched as the last two mails have been particularly large from my point of view as well as everyone else's so I think they must have been only delayed in the transmission and not sunk after all.

All is at peace again between the Commander and myself (his name is G.D. Stevenson, Mammy asked me in her last letter what it was). He has restored my camera to me and honours are easy so to speak. Not that a camera is much use now as we are having regular winter weather (and about time too) and we scarcely see the sun from days' end to days' end.

Last night we left Suvla for Mudros having been relieved by the Glory. That is the last we shall see of Suvla Bay for some time I expect as (the cat is out of the bag at last and the fell secret is no longer a "wichtiges geheimnis") after coaling and provisioning etc: at Mudros we are going back to Port Iero again! Most people are thoroughly fed up at going back to "that hole again" Certainly it is a dull hole to be in, but, like the wild wet cat in the Just So Stories, "all places are alike to me" and it doesn't worry me much where we go though it would have been rather decent to have gone to Salonika for a change. The Cornwallis is taking our place at Suvla and we are relieving the Euryalus at Iero while she goes to Malta. Our turn for Malta is next February.

We were making a hockey ground last time we were at Port Iero which we left to the Euryalus to finish. I wonder if they have finished it yet; if so we ought to be able to put in some decent games as we have all got sticks. We might even challenge the Frenchmen; that is to say if there is still a French ship there like there used to be.

Perhaps the captain will let us snotties go out in the patrol boats again like he did last time – you remember I was in the Rattlesnake, which bye the bye has gone home now – Personally I don't think its very likely though of course there's no knowing. Of course it wouldn't be half as decent now in winter-time as it was in the summer when last we were there but I think it would be better than sticking in the ship all the time.

I wish it were possible to send some of my trophies home as it would ensure them being safe, but the Post Office on board ship refuse to take them as it is strictly "verboten" to send anything in that line through the post so I just have to sit tight until the ship pays off when I will cart the whole caboodle along to adorn the ancestral halls and mantle-pieces.

Love to all from your affectionate son Philip.

Dec 7th, 1915
HMS Canopus, Port Iero

My dear Dad

I wish you a merry Christmas and hope you are in the best of health.

We are back again in Port Iero after a couple of months' absence. We got back last Thursday (I think it was) and as soon as the Euryalus had cleared out we moved up in her old billet. We haven't got so many anchors out as we had last time (the old Commander was dreadful in the way of anchors) but we can swing round head to wind instead of being quite stationary like we were last time which is always a good thing.

The next day a collier came alongside and we started to coal. As we had not coaled at Mudros this was a pretty lengthy operation; to be exact we had 1100 tons to come in.

However we were finished by 2.30 p.m. when the collier shoved off.

We found that in our absence the Euryalus had finished off all of the jobs which we had begun and made several other improvements such as pier-building etc: the chief thing was, however, that they had finished the hockey ground which we had begun. At first the captain would not give leave to anybody because he wanted to make quite certain what the attitude of the people ashore was to the British. Finding that they were quite friendly towards us, he gave short leave the next day to officers and men; but no one was allowed to go to Metylene. Immediately of course the men got up a football team and asked permission to go ashore and have a game which was granted.

Of course there was no one for them to play against, the Euryalus having left, so they just had to have a pick-up game amongst themselves. The next day the officers had the ground and so arranged a hockey games amongst themselves. Unfortunately I was not able to play as I had the afternoon watch. Apparently the ground is a very small one so although they only played 7 a side it did not seem too few. After the game a few energetic members of the gunroom had a bathe. They said the water wasn't very cold and I can quite believe them as the weather is very mild here and we are so landlocked we scarcely ever get any rough weather inside the harbour.

A trawler came in this morning bringing a mail for us. The rotten part about it is though that the trawler returns to Mudros at 4 p.m. this afternoon, therefore the mail for Mudros closes at 2 p.m. and as I had the forenoon watch (from 8.30 a.m to 12.30 p.m.) I have got to squash in all my Xmas letters to the family in 1 hour, allowing ½ an hour for dinner, which I am doing my best to do – hence my frantic haste. I only wish the trawler didn't shove off so soon.

By the time this letter reaches you I expect the Grecian question will have been settled, but at present it is in a most critical state, Of course the Greek people themselves are on our side but it is their king who is pro-German and who is trying to egg' them on into a war against England which would be most unpopular and probably lead to a revolution.

Hope you are quite fit – hurry up and send me that photo of yourself. Love from your affectionate son Philip.

Dec 7th, 1915
HMS Canopus, Port Iero

My dear Guy

I wish you a very happy Christmas and hope you are enjoying yourself.

There has been rather a bust-up here lately which I must tell you about.

Apparently at a place called Mosko Island, which is quite close to Aivali (the place of the mythical submarine which I wrote about ages ago) there has been a bit of a scrap. There are some Greek guards there who are supposed to look after the Greek inhabitants of Mosko Island which is a Turkish island. Well the other day some of the Greek guards (some of whom were in our pay) thought they would have a bit of fun, so they calmly murdered a few Turks who were living on this island and whom they did not like. The Turks (excluding the dead ones) replied by massacring all the Greeks they could lay hands on. Then a regular old fight began between the Turks and these Greek guards. Apparently the Greeks began to get rather the worst of it so they sent a deputy in the shape of an ancient and decrepit old priest to us to implore us to help his beloved people by sending them rifles as seeing that the people who started the whole show were in our pay, he considered it up to us to see them safely through it.

I don't know what the result of the conflab was but I think we did something to help them, anyhow the result was that the Gazelle brought off over 1000 Greek refugees from Mosko Island. Our Commander went along in a trawler to see what was going on, and, I think to direct operations. I don't know who won the fight, in fact for all I know it may still be going on now.

Anyhow I think it will have the effect of making the Greeks out here still more friendly with us as they consider we treated them handsomely. Things are going on here exactly the same as when we were last here. The snotties go out pulling every morning in the galley before breakfast the same as before, and everything else is the same.

Simply must stop now as mail is closing.

Love to all from Philip.

HMS Canopus
Port Iero
Dec 29th 1915

My dear Dad

Thank you very much for the £ 1 note which you sent me. This together with similar sums received from various relations and the accumulated arrears of pay which I haven't been able to spend much of add up to quite a considerable sum. Don't you think I ought to send some of it home to you to dispose of as you think fit. I think it would be rather decent if it was stuffed into a bank, and then it would be safer than sculling about the ship, and if we went to Malta or some place like that and I was short of cash, I could easily write home for some, or have a cheque book or something – in the approved style. Rather a high-class scheme don't you think?

Yesterday the "Ben-my-chree" which, before the war was an Isle of Man passenger boat, but has now been converted into a seaplane carrier had an evening show on to which the officers and a certain number of men from each of the ships in harbour were invited. It was a revue called "Here we are again". A lot of us went across to see it. The performance started at 8 and was held in the large space where their seaplanes are kept and was therefore an ideal place to hold a large audience.

It was an absolutely top-hole show. You would scarcely believe that it was wholly got together with material and labour on board ship. In one of the scenes a railway train came in. This was effected by a large wooden painted model with wheels which revolved and a most realistic effect was obtained by some people in the wings who made some extraordinary noises to represent the "puffs" and whistling etc.

A cinematograph was effected by the people on the stage acting the piece while over the stage a sort of muslin curtain was let down through which one could see. The "clicking" which always accompanies the working of a cinema was got by an electric fan, behind which a light was shining. Each blade of the fan lightly touched a piece of wood or something as it came round. This made the clicking. The light behind the fan threw a large shadow across the muslin giving a weird effect. It was jolly good. Also an aeroplane was forthcoming (in another scene) which was hoisted up in the air with a man inside it after which the propeller began whizzing round accompanied by the most realistic backfires and a continuous stream of puffs issued from the exhaust. The songs and choruses were also very good while all the actors were simply ripping. Altogether it was a most delightful show and it was close on midnight by the time we packed up and returned to the ship.

I was very pleased to get your photo. I thought it was awfully good – the best of the lot in fact.

I suppose you are being pretty hard worked at present with all your businesses as Jurat etc.

Our hockey ground is absolutely indispensable to us. We get some awfully good games on it. Also now that there has been a considerable addition to our little fleet here by the arrival of several new destroyers, we get different combinations in teams.

My new uniform from Gieve's arrived by last mail. It fitted me quite well although a trifle large. Also I got a cap and a few shirts, socks, cap-covers etc.

With best wishes for the New Year and best love to all those at home from

Your affectionate son Philip

> HMS Canopus
> Port Iero
> Jan 1st 1916

My dear Grandmamma

Thank you very much for the £1 note which you sent me for Christmas. There is not much opportunity for spending money in these parts but it will come in handy when we go to Malta or some fairly civilized place.

We had a children's party on board the other day and it was quite a novel entertainment. There are one or two English families living in Metylene, and some of our officers got to know these people and asked them to come over one day and bring their children with them. Unfortunately the kids were all the wrong age – most of them being about 2 years of age whilst the oldest was only 7. Still, we rigged up a few things for their amusement. There was a Father Christmas who dispensed presents, and a long sloping board for sliding down, also a *small go-cart drawn by the ship's goat and a basin of water containing a penny. Whoever tried to extract the penny got an electric shock which put them off rather successfully. A small play was acted in which a bear, a policeman and a tramp took a prominent part. I don't know what it was all about and I don't suppose any one else did either. There were a good many grown ups there too and a few nurses to look after the younger kids. On the whole I think it was quite a success.*

Last night, being New Year's Eve, I stayed up to see the New Year in. On these occasions, in the Service, all the officers gather round the ship's bell, while the youngest (usually of course a snotty) rings it, 16 times; 8 times for midnight of the old year and 8 times for midnight of the new year. Then they all join hands and sing "Auld Lang Syne" This time, however, we were much more sober. Only 2 officers from the wardroom turned up and not more than 4 from the gunroom. The bell was solemnly struck 16 times, and in hurried whispers we chanted Auld Lang Syne after which performance we all retired gloomily to our beds.

However I hope the New Year will bring us good luck and a definite offensive taken by the Allies in spite of the half-hearted way in which it was brought in on board H.M.S. Canopus.

We are having very fine weather here considering the time of year although of course we occasionally get heavy gales which are not at all pleasant. Still we are fairly safe from them in Port Iero.

I hope you are in the best of health. With much love from
Your affectionate grandson.
Philip

HMS Canopus
Jan 3rd 1916

My dear Dad

We have just discovered that our exams for acting subs come off next November (provided the war lasts up till then) Instant Panic!

Of course we will be a good deal behind the remainder of our term from the point of view of knowledge while we have been "strafing up the Dardanelles" they have been swotting in the North Sea. Still it now behoves us to make up for lost time by swotting for all we are worth. Hence we have started a systematic course of instruction, devoting one month at a time to each subject. To help me with my studies, I must ask you to send me the following books and instruments which I suppose you will find somewhere or other – I hope so anyway.

Seamanship Manual Vol1 (a blue book)
Pilotage Note-book (a long thin book full of pilotage notes)

Torpedo Manual Vol 1 (blue book-important)
Modern Engineering by Sennett and Oram (a fat green book)
Engineering Note-book (purple note-book containing engineering
sketches)
Box of Instruments (a decent thing with my name outside)
Sextant *
All old note-books such as electricity notebook, mechanics notebook
etc (ordinary note books generally with squared paper pages)
My schemes (a small green portfolio containing sheets of paper all
about Navigation)
Please take special care with my sextant as it is a very delicate
instrument. I suggest you give it to an instrument maker who will pack
it properly. I am awfully sorry for putting you to so much trouble on my
account but I have simply got to swot up and it is impossible without
all those books. I am sending 10/- for postage which will be heavy. A
wooden box would save all those books and instruments an awful lot of
knocking about.
I can't think of anything more I want, but I hope if I do discover
anything you will not mind me asking for it.
There is no news of any importance to tell you. We have got a few
suspected spies on board including two females.
Hope you are quite well
With much love to all from your affectionate son, Philip.

HMS Canopus
Port Iero
Jan 10th 1916

My dear Guy
I delayed writing you a letter in hopes that I would get one from you
about Christmas time which I would be able to answer. As evidently,
however, a mail must have been sunk at one time or another and with
it your letter, I am writing to you now to make up for lost time.
In about three weeks time we are going to bring out a small play
called "Hullo Everything" It is being got up by the Canopus' officers,
and no one else is going to take part in it except us. Not even the ship's
company. It has not quite matured yet, but evidently is going to be the
dream of a certain man called Gilbert the Filbert. Gilbert is really our
sub, Flynn. When the curtain rises, he is seen asleep in his bunk, while
his marine servant (another officer) is getting everything ready for him
getting up. However, he goes on sleeping and in the following scenes his
dream is acted. At one time history repeats itself when we act the capture

of the Austrian and German consuls by our landing parties in Metylene. At another time a Zeppelin comes over and drops bombs.

The scenes are being painted now. I have got two parts to play. At first I am a chorus-girl and join in all the choruses. Then afterwards I appear as a sailor in the landing party which is going to strafe the consuls in Metylene. I have already started by manufacturing my long hair to appear as a girl. This is being done by gumming and sewing a lot of tow (i.e. picked oakum) onto a cap-cover.

This looks quite effective. I have also made a long plat (zopf- ask Elie if you don't understand this) out of the same stuff. Then I have got to make myself a skirt and blouse (we have each got to make our own costumes). We are all allowed a certain amount of freedom in the way of acting little 'stunts' of our own. My 'stunt' will be to have a baby who will be fed from the spout for blowing up my Gieve waistcoat. As soon as the Zeppelins come flying over, however, I shall drop my baby and proceed to blow up my Gieve waistcoat for all I am worth at the same time dashing for cover – the whole idea is to make a fool of yourself for the amusement of the others. I hope the thing will be a success as it is entirely got up by amateurs, but I think it ought to be if everybody puts their hearts into it.

I have not yet thought of my rig as a sailor, but I should think that would be pretty easy to think out.

Hope you are all right
Love to all from Philip.

HMS Canopus
Port Iero
Feb 8th 1916

My dear Guy

Many thanks for your letter and also The Hound of the Baskervilles. *I read it once ages ago at Osborne but I shall enjoy reading it again very much. It is very exciting isn't it?*

There is a place called Thermi, quite close to here where there are a couple of French aeroplanes in an aerodrome. I believe it is quite easy to go up in one for the asking. I shall have a shot one day I expect and try my luck.

Most of our officers including the captain and commander have gone off to a small island called Long Island which is only a few miles from Smyrna to watch the building of a base for ships there. Also they are building an aerodrome there and when it is completed, all the aeroplanes at Thermi will be conveyed there where they will be used for spotting the fall of shot when our monitors start bombarding the

Smyrna forts which they will be doing pretty soon – in fact they are starting today I think.

There is absolutely nothing doing here now. Every day is exactly the same as the last.

Our leave had been stopped to Metylene for some reason or other but we are allowed there again now. That doesn't affect me much as I think Metylene is a frightful poky little hole and not worth going to.

We had a decent game of hockey yesterday; it is about the only thing which relieves the monotony of this place.

Personally I think it is awful rot starting swotting up for our exams already especially as they aren't coming off till November when we will probably be in different ships. Last mail I got a whole library of books from home which will come in very useful.

A whole party are going over to Thermi this morning – probably to have a shot at going up in an aeroplane if they can. Unfortunately none of us snotties will be able to go as of course we have our instructions to do.

Ellie apparently seems to be having a rare old time in her hospital what with night-duty etc: I got a letter from her saying that she was enjoying life very much.

I hope you are having a decent term of it with plenty of games etc; With much love to all from, Philip.

HMS Canopus
Port Iero
Feb 7th 1916

My dear Dad

Thank you very much for sending me my work books. I have received the following up to date:

Sennett and Oram
Torpedo Manual Vol 1
Seamanship Manual Vol 1

The rest are following on I expect. You were quite right about that small green portfolio. We used to call them schemes at Dartmouth – goodness only knows why.

I think it is rather rotten of the Admiralty. They force us poor snotties to have our sextants out here with us and yet they say definitely that they will give no compensation to any officer (except Navigating Officers) who loose their sextants on active service through a mail boat (or your own ship for that matter) being sunk.

Thanks awfully for making all those arrangements about my cash and the bank, so if ever you find some shekels enclosed in a letter you *know that they go to swell my banking account. We get paid once a month in the Service so you will expect my contribution then that is whenever I am flush of course.*

I asked our sub about Goddard's case and he said he didn't know there was any limit definitely laid down for remaining on the sick list before being invalided out of the service. Anyhow he has had a good long spell of leave hasn't he? About a year by now. His wrist doesn't hurt him at all I suppose does it?

They are sending all the cadets from Dartmouth now straight to the 1st or 2nd Battle Squadrons and the Battle Cruiser Squadrons as fast as they can. Personally I would just as soon be out here seeing what fun there is to be seen as in the Australia. Of course if the Germans ever try any more destructive raids on our East Coast, the Battle Cruisers would see all the fighting, but I think the German armoured cruisers and battle cruisers will lie low for a while after the maulings they have received at our hands. Of course the great advantage of a home station is that you get plenty of leave, though it must be awfully dull work patrolling.

I well remember the Australia when we were at Abrolhos Rocks. She arrived about 2 am one morning – we were guard ship and we challenged her by searchlight. She answered wrong. Our captain began to wonder at this but of course didn't do anything drastic as we knew for certain it was the Australia and not an enemy as we had been in communication with her for hours past by wireless. Eventually however it turned out that we had challenged wrongly and she had answered right; so our signal staff got strafed the more so than usual as the Australia was a flagship and so we had challenged the admiral wrongly.

She only stayed there a very short time however and we have not made her acquaintance since.

I got a letter from Ellie yesterday giving me an account of her life in the hospital and the night-work she did. She seems to be having a pretty strenuous time of it especially if she is on duty every night which I gather from her letter is the case. Still, she says she is enjoying herself which is the great thing.

I hope you and Mammy are quite well and the spring weather suits her.

With much love from your affectionate son, Philip.

Midshipman Philip Reginald Malet de Carteret (1898-1916)

HMMG Mary Rose
March 7th 1916

My dear Dad

I wish you many happy returns of the day and hope that you are quite well!

I am sending you a small souvenir of Anzac in the shape of a pencil made out of a Turkish bullet. I melted the inside of the bullet out which was only made of lead of course and then stuck the pencil in.

I suppose you have heard all about my going to the gun boat Mary Rose for a short time from Ellie to whom I gave an account of it. The very first day we were out on patrol we ran aground on some rocks to the south of Long Island, but I don't think we did much damage. However that night we had to take eleven Greek refugees back to Port Iero so we took the opportunity to stay there for a few days to carry out some minor repairs and fill up with stores and water etc. Also we asked the Canopus for a diver to examine our bottom and to remove a bit of rope which had become entwined around our propeller. In fact we stayed in Port Iero quite a long time, yesterday night being the first time we left it to return to Long Island. There wasn't much wrong with our bottom where we had touched – only a couple of sheets of copper plating scraped off which was soon put right by the divers. Our propeller was worse however and we had to have our stern hoisted out of the water to have a new one fitted on. The SNO gave orders that the place where we went ashore was to be buoyed as although it was 500 yards or so out from the shore yet there was only about three feet of water over it and any of the other gunboats might easily have gone ashore there.

Yesterday we spent most of the time running up and down between various places on Long Island on different errands. We visited Doctor's Island which is quite close to Long Island. The only reason I can think of why it is called Doctor's Island is because one of the monitor's doctors visits it periodically to attend to a sick Greek there. Still, the inhabitants of Doctor's Island always welcome the visits of the Gunboats and yesterday they gave us a large basket full of raisins. All these islands in the gulf of Smyrna abound with grapes and other fruit in season so of course there are always plenty of raisins when there are no grapes.

We also like these occasional visits to Doctor's Island as one can purchase young lambs there (slaughtered while you wait) which is about the only decent fresh meat you get.

Yesterday evening we escorted three French aeroplanes (I think I told you there is an aerodrome at Long Island) across to Smyrna on which they dropped bombs having previously dropped pamphlets on the same place written in Turkish enlarging on the futility of protracted hostilities against the allies (with a capital A) and how they (the

Turks of course not the Allies) were being thoroughly licked in every sphere of operations etc, etc, ad nauseam.

Just the sort of stuff they throw on us in fact. The aeroplanes returned all right but were followed shortly afterwards, scarcely visible in the gathering twilight by two Hun aeroplanes who flew calmly over the monitor lying at anchor in East Bay and dropped two eggs. They were contemplating dropping a few more but were driven off by the monitor's anti-aircraft guns.

After that we went to the North side of Doctor's Island where we anchored for the night, keeping watch. In the morning we shifted and went alongside the monitor lying in East Bay (Long Island) where we are lying at the present minute. I don't know what they will do with us to-day but we are due for a stand-off to-morrow.

I am sending you a fiver to stuff into the bank for me.

It is getting warmer every day – soon it will be warm enough to bathe. I tried yesterday but the water was pretty chilly.

With much love to all the family. From your affectionate son. Philip

P.S. Have just received M's letter. All serene about FI epistles.

HMMG Mary Rose
Long Island
March 22nd 1916

My dear Dad

There was a submarine scare yesterday. Apparently a hostile submarine has been sighted somewhere in the Metylene Channel which is between the island of Metylene and the mainland and about 30 miles North of Long Island. All the Motor Gunboats were called out to patrol various parts of the Gulf of Smyrna to try to prevent the submarine from getting through to Smyrna in case it wanted to.

This was rather bad luck on us as it happened to be our stand-off time but still it couldn't be helped. We had to go and anchor off the south of Doctor's Island and keep watch for the night. It was my first watch (8 pm to 12 midnight) and as a bright moon came out at about 9 pm we were able to see right across to the Turkish shore at Vourlah so provided a good look-out was kept the submarine could only get passed by sneaking along the Turkish coast with periscope awash. We had all our anti-submarine appliances ready. The bomb which you drag along on sighting a submarine was already for heaving overboard, 3 pdr guns *ready with night-sights shipped, rockets, Very's lights and searchlights all handy. Also we had to keep a wireless watch for the last quarter of every hour to pick up orders from the Senior Officer. Of course we all knew that nothing would happen and neither did it but still there is no harm in being prepared. Seeing that the whole of the Gulf of Smyrna is mined I should think that any ship would find it hard to get in unless they knew the minefields. Next morning we packed up our traps and shoved off back to Nikola (which is the name of our sort of base) to finish our stand-off. However we were not destined to have much peace for presently a SW gale sprang up, and as Nikola faces SW we didn't get much of a look in so we pulled up our mud-hook and skedaddled off round to East Bay where we spent an uncomfortable night rolling about due to a slightly choppy sea.*

This afternoon we go on patrol again. However we were cheered up by the arrival of our half-monthly stores from the Canopus the other day which included a small mail. It is lucky that you are addressing your letters to HMS Canopus and not to the Mary Rose as the poor Mary Rose hasn't had a mail for over three weeks. This is chiefly due to the fact that there is a destroyer called Mary Rose as well so those mails which belong to the Gunboat Mary Rose and are not sunk go to the destroyer Mary Rose. Conversely when we do get a mail it is half full of the other Mary Rose's letters.

The other day we got a large basket of back Press Messages which were very welcome as we hadn't had any war news for ages and in fact in this out-of-the-way corner of the world it is very hard to believe that we are at war at all. However things seem to be getting on all right and the Russians appear to be strafing the Turks pretty successfully.

Apparently that big German offensive at Verdun was a complete failure which is very satisfactory as it shows how well the French have got the situation in hand. I suppose we are simply waiting for favourable weather and opportunities before having a grand Big Push on every front. That ought to shake the Huns alright.

I don't think there is any more news to tell you
With love from your affectionate son. Philip.

Royal Navy Barracks
Chatham
Sunday Evening

My dear Dad
We arrived at Chatham at about 3 o'clock on Sunday morning. Not a soul expected us or had been told we were going to come. Of all the

biggest blunders I have ever met, the Admiralty really are the worst. Not a single ship which we had been sent to join was at Chatham or anywhere near there. The authorities at Chatham contemplated sending us straight back to Dartmouth, but eventually put us up for the remainder of the night in a large gymnasium belonging to the barracks.

Next morning or rather the same morning, we learnt that the Canopus was in Devonport which is a considerable distance the other side of Dartmouth!

We went to church in the morning, and at 2.15 in the afternoon several cadets went off to their ships which were in Sheerness. I think that they are going to send us off to Devonport to-morrow morning, but one cannot tell for certain as this is the most weird place I have ever met – as soon as an order is given it is immediately changed in favour of another one which in turn succumbs to a third. Still, they are giving us quite a good time here – nothing to do, good food and a ripping swimming bath.

Our chests are going to be left at the barracks while we go to our ships, and we are each taking a 'ships bag' into which every article we want to take on board is crammed and a hammock. I think that letters addressed to HMS Canopus c/o GPO ought to reach me, that is, if we are going to our ships tomorrow which I cannot guarantee for certain but nevertheless seems probable. Not a word has been spoken about leave – I shall probably not get any for ages – it's too sickening.

I can't make out what possessed the Admiralty to send 140 cadets to Chatham when there is not a single ship in the place. I hear that they have been making futile attempts to stop the special train ever since it left Dartmouth, practically the Canopus, being in the third fleet, will not be joining the fighting line and will hence not join in a pitched battle but will be engaged in convoy duty or something.

I hope you are all quite well.

With love to all from your affectionate son. Philip.

Captain Harold Ackroyd VC, MC, MD, RAMC (1877-1917)

With contributions from Christopher Ackroyd, grandson

O N the 11 August 1917, a German sniper's bullet prematurely ended the life of Harold Ackroyd. He was going about his normal daily business of attending to the wounded men of his battalion dodging from shell-hole to shell-hole in the front line. According to his batman, Pte A. Scriven, who was in charge of the Advanced Dressing Station that day, Harold was about 150 yards in front of him visiting each company and attending to the wounded, when he was shot through the head by a sniper. Scriven didn't actually witness the deed, but says that upon hearing the news,

Portrait of Harold - London, 1916
(author)

"I immediately took a party of stretcher- bearers, but on arrival found that he was dead. There were six other poor fellows in the same shell-hole who had met the same fate; it was a perfect death trap".

EARLY LIFE

Harold Ackroyd was born on 18th July 1877 in Southport, Lancashire and his family first lived at 26 Roe Lane (later renumbered as 134) before moving to 'Mulhacen', 8 Morley Road. Both houses have now been demolished. He was baptised on 29th August 1877 in St Cuthbert's Church North Meols. This church is known as the Mother Church of Southport as it was the first church in the town dating from 1178. He was the youngest son of the six children of Edward Ackroyd, who had made his living from textiles and became Chairman of The Southport & Cheshire Lines Extension Railway Co. His mother Ellen Holden, was from a wealthy Bolton family. Two of the six children died in early childhood, before Harold was born, and a sister, Elizabeth died in 1914, leaving an elder sister, Annie and an older brother, Edward. Robert Holden, Harold's maternal grandfather was a cotton waste dealer in Bolton, who had made a considerable fortune. On the death of his wife Anne in 1878, the considerable inheritance passed to their daughter, Ellen, Harold's mother. This change of fortune allowed Harold's father, Edward to assume a significant place in Southport society, allowing him to give his two sons Edward and Harold a private education.

Harold was an intelligent boy and after "Mintholme" preparatory school in Southport he went to AF Chance's House at Shrewsbury School in the Easter term 1891 and left in the summer of 1896. This later became Severn Hill House. He then followed his brother Edward and gained a place at Gonville & Caius College (1896-1899), Cambridge. He completed his BA in 1899 and continued his studies at Guy's Hospital, achieving his MB, BS in 1904 and finally gaining an MD in 1910.

Shrewsbury School, OTC – 1894
Harold is in 2nd Row – 2nd from the right (CEA)

Harold had hospital appointments at Guy's Hospital, the General Hospital in Birmingham and the David Lewis Northern Hospital in Liverpool. It is possible that Harold moved back to Cambridge in 1907 to

Freshers at Gonville & Caius College, Cambridge, 1896.
Harold is front row, 2nd from the Left (CEA)

Gonville & Caius College, Cambridge – 1st Lent, 1897.
Harold is seated front row, 2nd from the right (CEA)

work on a voluntary basis at the Strangeways research hospital where he met his met his future wife, Mabel Smythe, who was said to be the matron. After this he secured a British Medical Association Research Scholarship in 1908 and became a research scholar attached to Professor WE Dixon`s Laboratory in the department of Pharmacology at the Downing Site Laboratories where Dixon was at the time a lecturer. His initial work was into Purine metabolism and he published six papers in the Biochemical Journal. "On the presence of Allantoin in certain foods" 1911 (1) and "On Purine metabolism of Rats" 1914 (2). He later joined the newly founded Institute for the study of Animal Nutrition, Department of Agriculture and worked with Sir Frederick Gowland Hopkins, the first Professor of Biochemistry at Cambridge who went on to win a Nobel Prize in 1929 for his pioneering research into the discovery of vitamins. Harold's last paper published in 1916 was actually written by Sir Frederick. "Feeding experiments with deficiencies in the amino-acid supply: Arginine and Histidine as possible precursors of Purines." 1916 (3). In the introduction there was a generous tribute to Harold.

> *"Several of the experiments described in this paper were made in 1914 and the rest in 1915. My colleague has been long at the front, and in writing the paper I have been unable to consult him. He has had moreover no opportunity of reviewing the experimental results as a whole. If therefore it be held that the conclusions are not warranted by the facts I am alone responsible. FGH."*

Harold and Mabel were married on 1st August 1908 at All Saints Church in Southport and they had three children; Ursula (14/06/1909) (my grand-

Guys Hospital Staff, 1905 Harold is in the 2nd row, fourth from the left (CEA)

Harold as a Houseman at Guys Hospital in 1905 (CEA)

mother), Stephen (29/04/1912) and finally Anthony (Tony) (20/10/1914). The family first lived in Great Shelford and then in 1912 they moved to Brooklands, 46 Kneesworth Street, Royston, Hertfordshire. Harold travelled to work in Cambridge by train, motor bike and eventually in a Morgan three wheeler car..

Harold had independent private means and probably did not have to engage in regular medical practice. We believe he travelled widely in Europe between 1905 and 1910 and spoke German well and also visited the Amazon and Japan. His brother, Edward, who was two years older, was also academic, winning a Scholarship to Gonville & Caius, Cambridge. He subsequently read for the Bar becoming a barrister and had chambers at Lincoln's Inn.

Harold's colleague, Sir Frederick Gowland Hopkins, wrote these words about him in his Obituary published in the Biochemical Journal of 1918:

Royston War Memorial (author)

*Harold &
Mabel Royston,
1915
(Genette
Dagtoglou)*

*Harold &
Mabel Royston,
1916
(Genette
Dagtoglou)*

*Harold Ackroyd
in garden at
Royston,
(Genette
Dagtoglou)*

Captain Harold Ackroyd VC, MC, MD, RAMC (1877-1917)

'Brooklands', 46 Kneesworth Road, Royston, Cambs (author)

Harold at Brooklands, Royston
(C MdeC)

Harold & Ursula at Brooklands, Royston
(CMdeC)

6th Battalion, Royal Berkshire Regiment – sometime mid 1916 – before 1/7/1916. Back Row – Left To Right 2/Lt Broadley, 2/Lt A. Jackson, 2/LT Spencer, 2/Lt L.A. Kingham, Capt. J.N. Richardson, 2/Lt A.A. Barrett, Lt. H.S. Tindall, Rev C. Parkinson, Lt. Battans, Lt. R.E. Kemble, Lt. Wrinham, Lt. Joseph. Front Row – Left To Right Capt. N.B. Hudson, Capt. H.G.F. Longhurst, Maj. Goldsmith, Lt.Col. B.G. Clay, Capt. R.A. Rochfort (Adjutant), Lt R.M. Guthrie (Quarter Master), Capt. H. Ackroyd (IWM)

"He hesitated a good deal before deciding to devote himself entirely to scientific research though so well qualified to do it. He was fond of travel and had a passion for the sea. While undecided about his career he indulged in these tastes freely, going for long voyages in slow boats and exploring Europe pretty thoroughly. He attached himself first to the Department of Pharmacology, and afterwards to the School of Agriculture where he accepted a post in the newly founded Institute for the study of Animal Nutrition. He had previously held for some time a British Medical Association Scholarship. He concerned himself chiefly with the subject of purine metabolism. For a long time while at the School of Agriculture he engaged most patiently in a laborious study of the nitrogenous constituents of root-crops. A few months before the War, (in the summer of 1914) I proposed to him some conjoint work upon possible precursors of purines in the body. He began the work, and a preliminary paper was published in December, 1916 – a paper which unhappily Ackroyd never saw. To one who knew him best as a colleague patiently engaged in details of laboratory work these eloquent words (the VC citation) bring a strange sense of contrast. Ackroyd however brought courage to every task and did everything well".

Captain Harold Ackroyd VC, MC, MD, RAMC (1877-1917)

WAR

War was declared on 4th August 1914 and the British Expeditionary Force was sent to France. The British Army was a professional force and had less than 80,000 men, They faced a German disposition of over one million men. At the Battle of Mons on 23rd August the British Army was forced to make a tactical retreat. The situation was saved by the combined armies of the French and British with over one million men at the Battle of the Marne which took place between 5th - 12th September. It became clear that the War would not be over quickly and both sides dug in for the prolonged trench war of the western front. Field Marshal Lord Kitchener started his vigorous recruitment campaign for his new volunteer Armies. The war dragged on into 1915 and recruitment fervor reached new heights. Although Harold was aged thirty-seven and had no recent experience of acute medical or accident work and was working as a research scientist he decided to volunteer and was commissioned as Temporary Lieutenant on the 15th February 1915. He was attached as Medical Officer to the 6th Battalion Royal Berkshire Regiment, which formed part of the 53rd Infantry Brigade in the 18th Division. After training at camps in Colchester and Codford St. Mary on the edge of Salisbury Plain, the Division sailed for France on 25th July 1915.

"The Regiment was posted opposite Carnoy & Fricourt on the Somme Front and took over a portion of the Front Line held by the 5th Division on 22 August. By the end of 1915, the Division had suffered 1,247 casualties, the quietest four months in its history." (4)

On 15th February 1916, Harold was promoted to Temporary Captain. During the first half of 1916 there was a stalemate between the Allies and the German forces. Harold was on leave at Bray from 7th until 20th April. There are twenty-two letters that Harold wrote to his daughter Ursula all in pencil, which give some idea of conditions at the front, though Harold spares the gruesome detail. Strangely they only begin in May, 1916. Sadly there are none written to Mabel which survive.

17/5/16
B.E.F.
France

Dear Ursula
I was very pleased to get your letter and to hear you are all quite well. At present I am living in a small village where we can not hear any guns or banging noises. We have not been so quiet since we came to France.

It is really very nice but I expect it won't last long.

Tell mother I got the parcel of food quite safely and also the clothing.

Much love to you and mother and Stephen and Anthony

Your loving father

Harold Ackroyd

31/5/16

B.E.F

France

Dear Ursula

I am glad to hear you got my letter quite safely. It had such a long way to go to get to you and might have got lost.

You would think it so funny if you could see the house I am writing in all underground and with no windows; but we have a door – it is a very good house – and when we open the door it lets the light in so I can see to write. Another man and myself both live in it and we have beds with wire on instead of a mattress. It is hard at first but one is soon used to it and it is much better than sleeping on the ground.

I forgot to tell you it has a brick floor taken from other houses because all the ordinary houses where we are have been knocked down by the naughty Germans.

And all the time there are banging noises – made I am glad to say mostly by our side not as it used to be.

Your loving father

Harold Ackroyd

7/6/16

Dear Ursula

I am not now in that nice underground house I wrote to you about but about 4 miles back in a little town – full of soldiers some of them brown from India, some English, some French – all sorts of languages. Now I live in a barn, with a biscuit box to sit on and a bed made of sacking; but the roof does not leak and the place is dry. I was in the same town last September. We get very good food indeed but fetch everything from another town as far away from here as you are from Cambridge but there is no nice train to take you.

Perhaps I shall be able to come home to see you in about six weeks but we can never tell

Much love to you and Stephen and Anthony

Your loving father

Harold Ackroyd

PS please ask mother to send me a cake of Pears soap. H.A.

Captain Harold Ackroyd VC, MC, MD, RAMC (1877-1917)

21/6/16

Dear Ursula

I was so glad to hear that you had a good birthday and lots of presents.

At present I am very busy and have not much time to write so please tell mother that my letters may be less frequent even than usual but she must not worry about that as I am quite well.

Much love to all the children
Your loving father
Harold Ackroyd

1st DAY OF THE SOMME – 1st JULY , 1916

The most intense fighting was between the French and Germans at Verdun and it became necessary to relieve the pressure on the French Army. It was decided that there should be a strategic offensive to draw the Germans away from Verdun. After an eight day artillery barrage of 1,600,000 shells, the British and Allied infantry advanced on the morning of the 1st July and by evening had suffered the largest loss sustained by the British army in a single day. 57,470 casualties including 19,240 killed.

> *"The 6th Royal Berkshires were immediately in front of Mine Trench, the most advanced of the enemy defences at the start of the day. At the west end of the trench was Casino Point, under which a British mine was exploded at 7.27am with disastrous effects on the enemy. A machine gun firing right on top of the mine was blown up and found some forty yards away. The falling debris caused slight loss among the Battalion, but, on the other hand, as they advanced three minutes after the explosion, Germans came forward with their hands up to surrender. After the capture of Mine Trench, the Battalion captured Pommiers Trench and Loop Trench." (5)*
>
> *"At Pommiers Redoubt Colonel BG Clay (commanding) and Captain R.A Rochfort (Adjutant) visited the line, where a German Officer had a shot at them and his bullet went through the right-hand pocket of the Colonel's jacket. It annoyed him very much, as it was a new "Fielding" jacket which he had just brought back with him from England. Later that day, Colonel Clay accused me of treading on his heels when I was about five yards away from him, but later discovered that a bullet had gone clean through the leather block of his heel.(from Captain Rochfort's Diary)" (6)*
>
> *"It was not until 6.30pm that the final objective, on a line running east and west in front of Caterpillar Valley, was reached. The enemy had*

93

been driven back from a depth of about two thousand yards of trenches on this day, but at a very heavy cost in officers and men. Seven officers had been killed and five wounded including Captains V.G. McArthur and H.G.F. Longhurst. 56 other ranks had been killed, 237 wounded and 46 missing." (7)

"By 8.00pm the Division had received a congratulatory telegram from General Congreve commanding the X111 Corps. General Ivor Maxse added "Well done, it's what I expected. Now hold on to what you have gained so splendidly". 695 prisoners had been captured and the Division suffered 3,707 casualties." (8)

"The advance of the 18th Division on the first day of the Battle of The Somme had been one of the few successes.

The Battalion was relieved on 2nd July by the 8th Suffolks and returned to Carnoy where they stayed until 7th July. They rested and helped clear the battlefield until the 7th." (9)

Harold's letter to Ursula from the rest area away from the front of 9th July 1916, describes how the battalion fared.

Dear Ursula, Mother will have told you many things that have happened here and I could tell you more, but the less said the better. The battalion I am with did splendidly and now is with them a few miles to recoup and refit. A few days ago where we are was under constant fire but now is as safe as Royston though in the distance we hear guns always firing and everywhere are funny balloons watching the enemy. Tell mother that daddy is very well and very happy though there is much to make one sad.

We were right in the middle of the first day's great fight and our battalion was in the front line. I can tell you I was very proud of the officers and men I have known so long. Now we rest on what a few days ago was a bare hill side – nothing but mud – now covered with funny little shelters against the wind and rain and we are all very happy and contented sleeping on the ground while at last the sun shines and it does not rain. You would be so interested to see it all with funny little cages for the German prisoners to stay in for a few hours before leaving for England. Give my love to mother and the boys.

Your loving father, Harold Ackroyd

DELVILLE WOOD

By 17th July, the British had a tenuous hold on a ridge whose high point was the salient of Delville Wood, which had been the scene of desperate fighting.

It is necessary to explain the 53rd Brigade's part in the fight to hold Delville Wood, in order to give the details of the action for which Harold was to receive 11 recommendations for the Victoria Cross. He was later to be awarded the Military Cross for this action. Delville Wood was to prove to be the graveyard of the 53rd Brigade

The 6th Royal Berkshire's strength for the attack was nineteen officers and four hundred and one men.

On the morning of the 19th July under the command of Brigadier-General Higginson the Brigade fought its way into the southern half of the wood where the South Africans had been forced out. For two days and two nights they remained dug in and held the ground they had gained against furious and continuous counter attacks and under appalling shell fire.

"The general scheme for the recapture of the wood was as follows. The 8th Battalion Norfolk Regiment was to clear the wood south of Princes Street – a drive that ran east to west through the wood and as soon as this was done, the other three battalions of the Brigade were to attack northwards – the 10th Essex on the right and the 6th Royal Berks in the centre. The 8th Suffolks were to clear Longueval on the left. It was arranged that the O.C. of the Norfolks should inform Brigade Headquarters of the hour at which he would be ready for the artillery barrage to be put on. The hour was provisionally settled for 6.15 a.m. on 19 July, but subsequently this had to be altered, and it was not until 7.15 a.m. that the attack could be launched. A message to this effect was sent to Brigade Headquarters, but it was not received until 7.51 a.m., consequently no artillery support was arranged for, and the attack proceeded without it. There was only one entrance into the wood on the south side, and the way from Longueval to this entrance was under direct machine-gun fire, which became so intense that the Norfolks, who were in front, could not at first get into the wood, although subsequently they managed slowly to clear the ground south of Princes Street and work as far eastwards as Buchanan Street. The 6th Royal Berkshires lost 34 men before getting into Longueval." (10)

GALLING FIRE

"The holding up of the Norfolks delayed the 10th Essex, who were behind them. Colonel Scott commanding the 10th Essex pushed on

through the Norfolks with his Battalion headquarters party and got into the wood. His signaling officer, Lieut. E. Bird, was shortly instructed to join him in the wood with six runners. There was such a galling fire to be passed through at the cross-roads at Longueval that Lieut. Bird arrived with only one runner, two had been killed and three wounded. The other battalions followed the Norfolks and the Essex into the wood and the men had to run in singly under withering machine-gun fire and shelling, which increased in intensity once the attack had been launched. Capt A.H. Hudson, who was at that time a company commander with the Berkshires said, "I did not, however, see a single man falter". The tremendous shell-fire, having cut off the battalions from communication with Brigade Headquarters, prompted General Higginson to send Maj. J.C. Markes, his Brigade Major, and Lieut. Neild, the Brigade Intelligence Officer, to investigate the situation. Major Markes was, however, hit in the chest and killed soon after passing through Longueval." (11)

"The fighting was of confused and individual nature that had characterised the struggle in Trones Wood. The Norfolks pushed on east of Buchanan Street and a considerable number of the enemy were killed by Lewis Guns and grenades, the remainder retiring to the south-east corner of the wood. By 1.30 p.m. the Norfolks had cleared the whole of the wood south of Princes Street, and the Essex, Berkshires and Suffolks started to attack northwards. Little progress was made with this advance owing to the exceedingly heavy machine-gun fire, and at 5 p.m. all four battalions were ordered to halt where they were and dig in. In Longueval the Suffolks had not been able to progress farther than the crossroads in the middle of the village. The portion of the line held by the 6th Royal Berkshires was manned by about 240 rifles, 6 Lewis guns and 4 Vickers guns." (12)

"So the battalions dug themselves in, and for two nights held onto what they had gained. It was two days and two nights of the grimmest kind of warfare, for the German shelling did not cease, and the enemy poured in reinforcements in a desperate attempt to recapture the stretch of the tangled undergrowth and shell-smitten trees that they had lost." (13)

HEAVY CASUALTIES

"The wood was littered with hundreds of wounded and dying men; South Africans, men of 53rd Brigade as well as Germans. Colonel Scott was hit in the head by a piece of shell and was caught by the Adjutant,

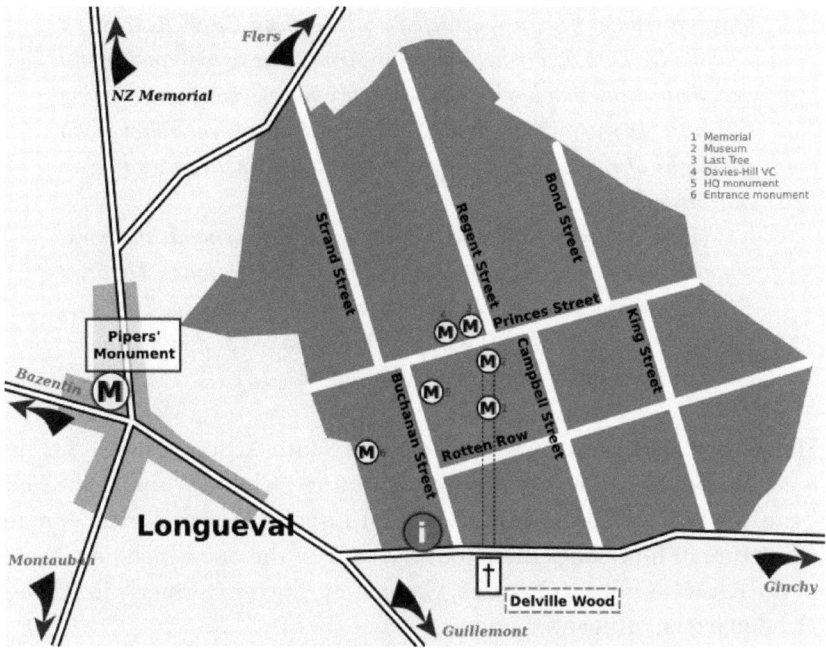

Capt. R.A. Chell, as he fell down the steps of the dug-out; Lieut. J.D. Archibald of the Essex was mortally wounded; and Lieuts. Byerley, Bird and Pinder-Davis were hit. The 10th Essex lost 200 other ranks in this engagement and the other battalions of the Brigade lost as heavily. While Capt Hudson of the Berkshires, wearing a private's uniform, was talking to the Regimental Sergeant-Major, a German sniper saw them and killed the Sergeant-Major. Capt. Hudson had a further escape when a bullet passed through his tin hat. The 6th Berkshires had one of their battalion taken prisoner for the first time in the war. They claim that they only lost nine men in that way during the whole war. The casualties of the 6th Royal Berkshires were 2 Officers killed, 5 wounded, 2 missing. 21 other ranks killed, 126 wounded and 29 missing – i.e. 44% of the Battalion." (14)

Captain Arthur Hensley Hudson would be killed at Passchendaele on 31st July, 1917. His brother Noel was also in the 6th Battalion. He later won the DSO and bar and became Lt. Colonel in command of the 8th Battalion. After the war became Bishop of Ely.

"Capt. Ackroyd, the Medical Officer of the Berks, was a heroic figure during those two days. The fighting was so confused and the wood so hard to search that the difficulty of evacuating the wounded seemed

unconquerable. The, bespectacled and stooping Capt. Ackroyd, a Cambridge Don before he joined the Army, was so cool, purposeful and methodical, that he cleared the whole wood of wounded, including German. It was a shattered 53rd Brigade that was relieved on the night of the 21-22 July by the 4th Royal Fusiliers and other Battalions". (15)

"The whole of Delville Wood was not yet in British hands and it was almost a month before it was completely cleared of Germans. The 53rd Brigade managed to hang on to the ground it had gained. The losses sustained during the battle were 12 Officers killed and 39 wounded, and 181 other ranks killed and 773 wounded." (16)

Harold had rescued many wounded of the South African Brigade, and he is remembered in the room commemorating Delville Wood at the Fort Beaufort Historical Museum, near East London, South Africa. A matt oil picture of him hangs there today, a copy of the one which now hangs in the RAMC Officers Quarters, Camberley, Surrey (formerly in RAMC Headquarters, Millbank, London)

Harold wrote the following letters home after the battle:

23/7/16

Dear Ursula and Stephen

Many thanks for your birthday present and wishes. I should so like to be able to come and see you.

The places I have been in lately are so very noisy but now it is all quiet and peaceful and perhaps I may get leave to come home before long so as to see you.

Your loving father
Harold Ackroyd

27/7/16

Dear Ursula

I am so glad to hear you like Cornwall; is not it nice down by the sea? I do so wish that I could come over to see you but I am afraid that it is not likely that I shall get home for some time. Won't it be jolly when Father comes home for good and there is no more war; though I am afraid you and I will not be able to go for any more rides together in the motor because after this war no one will be able to keep motors I expect.

I am now in such a nice quiet country place where you would hardly believe there was a war at all except that in the distance we can hear the guns. I don't suppose we shall stay here very long but shall soon go up nearer those same guns and hear their louder roar. But you know we get used to hearing banging noises as you are now to hearing the sea at night so it does not worry us at all.

It is only when the noises come and bang very close that it is unpleasant and then well it is very nasty but they won't hurt your daddy.

Much love to you, Stephen and Anthony.

Your loving father

Harold Ackroyd

28/7/16

Dear Ursula

I was glad to hear from mother that you were so good at the Dentists. Fancy a little girl like you having all those teeth stopped.

Jock is very well he has just returned from his leave last night; he has been 10 days in England and had his M.C. presented by the King.

Will you ask Mother to send me all those army maps I brought home when I was ill – they are in the lower drawers of my writing desk.

Much love to all

Your loving father

Harold Ackroyd

Delville Wood Communications Trench July 1916, (IWM – Q4417)

SICK LEAVE

On 11th August 1916 Harold returned to England on sick leave. He was given six weeks to recover by the Army Medical Board and he went to Cornwall to convalesce with the family. A posthumous letter written to Mabel from Alfred J. Clark dated 13th August, 1917 reveals;

"We were all half sorry when he returned after getting blown up last July, for we knew that if he came back, he would go on taking appalling risks and that the end was almost a certainty, he of course knew this equally well."

This confirms that Harold indeed was injured in some way because when he returned to the front he took to wearing goggles. It is very likely that he was suffering from exhaustion after the awful experience of being under continuous shell fire in Delville Wood while rescuing the wounded.

He seems to have recovered quickly because in a letter to his brother, Edward, dated 4th September, he says,

"I am now quite well and am really quite fit to return to duty but the Medical Board insisted on giving me 6 weeks sick leave of which I have still nearly 5 to serve. I argued with them that 10-14 days would be quite enough with the result that they got shirty and said I must take what the Board gave me; an awful lot of old fossils. I would hate the battalion to go into action without me."

Harold was passed fit for service on 3rd October and on the 20th he was awarded the Military Cross for his actions in Delville Wood.

"For conspicuous gallantry and devotion to duty during operations. He attended the wounded under heavy fire, and finally, when he had seen that all our wounded from behind the line had got in, he went out beyond the front line and brought in both our own and enemy wounded, although continually sniped at."

He returned to France in November, but was not back with the Battalion until December.

Here are Harold's remaining letters written home in 1916:

> *Nov 6th 1916*
> *S.M.O(?)*
> *Harfleur*
> *B.E.F. France*

Dear Ursula

I was so glad to get your two letters. What a splendid time you must have had in London.

I am still here far away from where I want to see the places again which you will see on the pictures.

Tell Mother she can send anything on to me here as they will be forwarded alright and at present there is no news of a move.

Much love to my little girl and to mother and Stephen and Anthony.
Your loving father
Harold Ackroyd

> *Nov 20th 1916*

Dear Ursula

I have just got your letter and was so pleased to get it as I had not heard from anyone for such a long time.

Won't you be sorry that Gertrude is going away and I am sure poor old Dick will be.

It has been so very cold here and the wind has been terrible but it is warmer now and wet again.

I hope you tried to comfort mother well on her Birthday. Although you don't get presents then.

Much love little Girl
Your loving father
Harold Ackroyd

> *Dec 12, 1916*
> *6th Bn R. Berks*
> *B.E.F. France*

Dear Ursula

I was so pleased to get a letter from you – what a funny thing to drop your teeth about. It is better than having them pulled out.

I am now back with my old regiment but we are resting so I am not in the trenches at present. It has been snowing quite a lot here and the snow is now melting.

Much love
Your loving father
Harold Ackroyd

1917

Here are Harold's letters written home before the 3rd Battle of Ypres (Passchendaele) which commenced on the 31st July.

7/1/17

Dear Ursula

I was so glad to get your letter from Brighton telling me how much you enjoyed yourself there. I do wish I could have been with you.

You must be a very good girl while I am away and help mother by being very nice to Stephen and every one else. You know how much I like to hear people say you are a good little girl.

Much love
Your loving father
Harold Ackroyd

18/1/17

Dear Ursula

I was very pleased to get your letter and so glad you like Brighton.

If mother has bought you a goldfish you must be very kind to it and feed it every day and give it water or it will die.

I have never seen the little airships you saw, they must be very scary!

I am sleeping out in a tent with snow all round and about 100 yards away is a great big balloon. I am very happy now I am back with my battalion.

Much love
Your loving father
Harold Ackroyd

Harold and unknown by barrage balloon – date unknown (CMdeC)

Captain Harold Ackroyd VC, MC, MD, RAMC (1877-1917)

26th February, 1917

Dear Ursula

I was very pleased to get the photographs they really are quite good.

I was glad to get your letters they are very interesting and tell me all about home.

I wish I could tell you of some of the interesting things out here but it is not allowed; mother will see it all in the newspaper and tell you all about.

Your loving father
Harold Ackroyd

Dear Ursula

This is one of the field post cards the German soldiers send home to their little girly.

I found it just near here in a field full of little pits and any amount of queer shaped iron things (shells) lying about.

The grass is now just showing green in those fields and very nice it looks after the brown desolation.

Your loving father
Harold Ackroyd

16/3/17

Dear Ursula

I was very pleased with your letter. How funny of Mother to forget Dick's hand?

You know I told you about the funny brown fields with holes full of water – well they now look quite green with grass in places and you can imagine how glad we all are to see it; and over there we hope to find real fields and villages before long. Here where we are all the villages have fallen down and all the time there are funny banging noises which I think must have something to do with the houses falling and when those banging noises stop father will probably come home for good.

Meanwhile the naughty Germans are running away just now, but they are very mischievous and set traps for nice British soldiers but they get more than they give.

Much love
Your loving father
Harold Ackroyd
P.S. Did you get my German postcard.

24/3/17

Dear Ursula

I was very pleased to get your letter and the beautiful painting.

We have now come back a bit into a somewhat dirty country village and are wandering about the country.

But it is all very peaceful and quite a pleasant change, though I am really sorry not to see more of the land our division has done to win back. Some day I will tell you all about it – after the war.

Much love
Your loving father
Harold Ackroyd

10/4/17

Very many thanks to all you kids for the chocolate you sent for Easter
Dear Ursula

I was sorry to hear that Stephen has hurt himself – I do hope it is not bad.

The German cap was taken in Irles, a few hours after the English entered and the two belts just after the Battle of Miraumont on Feb 17th. I have a whistle. I will send you some tins (?) that I found lying in the street about three hours after we took a village it must be a German one.

Much love
Your loving father
Harold Ackroyd

22/4/17

Dear Ursula

I was very glad to get your last letter.

I expect that you will be able to talk French quite well when I come home, but that will not be for quite a long time I am afraid.

It does seem such a long time since I was last at home.

It is now quite warm and spring seems to have really come at last. I expect the garden is beginning to look very nice now.

Much love
Your loving father
Harold Ackroyd

16/5/17

Dear Ursula

Yes I have received your letters and very glad to get them. I am very sorry that I cannot get you any stamps at present.

The weather here is splendid as warm as in summer, but cold at night.

I should like to see the garden at home.

Your loving father

Harold Ackroyd.

8/6/17

Dear Ursula

I hope this letter will reach you in time for your birthday to wish you many happy returns. I have not been able to get you many stamps but send you what I have. They are mostly English but a few American, South African and Canadian.

The weather here is very hot with a few heavy showers of rain.

I am sure you will enjoy Devonshire and I do wish I could come and see you there.

Much love

Your loving father

Harold Ackroyd.

17/6/17

Dear Ursula

I was so pleased to get your letter it was so nice of you to get the four leaved clover and send it to me. I am sure it will bring me luck and the first piece of luck I hope from it is that soon I may get leave home for a few days but that of course is not settled yet.

Yes Jock does smoke cigarettes but I don't know what kind and it is no good sending him a kind he does not like.

It is very hot here and we are back in a peaceful village several miles away from the fighting.

We got here yesterday after a very hard march and have been trying to keep cool ever since.

Much love

Your loving father

Harold Ackroyd

18TH DIVISION

The engagements of the Division between September 1916 and July 1917 were numerous and included Thiepval, and the Schwaben Redout, The Ancre, Boom Ravine, Irles and Cherisy. The Division saw a good deal of the fiercest fighting during the whole war. It was now attached to General Jacob's II Corps of Sir Hubert Gough's Fifth Army.

> *"Only those who fought through and survived the Flanders summer and autumn campaigns of 1917 probed the war's awfulness to its depths. From the beginning of the battle that became to be known as Passchendaele, until the taking of that village on 6 November, British losses totalled 268,000 men." (17)*
>
> *"July 1917 was a month of preparation for the offensive in Flanders. The 53rd Brigade was to spearhead the attack by the 18th Division. During the month they remained in training at Steenvorde, finding billets in farm buildings. Trips were made to a field between Ouderdom and Poperinghe where a vast model of the area to be attacked had been prepared and many explanatory lectures were given regarding the battle tactics. The barrage of shell-fire by the Germans persisted during the build up. Out of the 2,000 men of the 54th and 55th Infantry Brigades engaged in digging, and fetching and carrying in the preparing of the front-line system, the losses sustained during the eighteen days of preparation were terrible. 9 Officers and 171 other ranks were killed and 29 Officers and 655 other ranks were wounded of which ninety-five per cent of the casualties were caused by shell-fire." (18)*

Harold's last known letter, written to Ursula on the 19th July doesn't mention anything of the forthcoming 3rd Battle of Ypres.

> *Dear Ursula, I was so pleased to get your letter today. It is really so nice for you to be able to write all by yourself. I suppose you have got the letters which I sent home on the way and when I got back to the battalion they are still where I found them in quite a peaceful village where one might easily believe there was no war on. Tell mother that a year ago today we were in Delville Wood; it was such a dreadful place and now a year later all is quiet and peaceful. I did remember my birthday although I was not at home and thought of you all. Tell mother that I received the clothes and the cake and will write to the bank. I suppose today you are on the way down to Devon. I do hope you have a good time. Much love to you all.*
>
> *Your loving father. Harold Ackroyd*

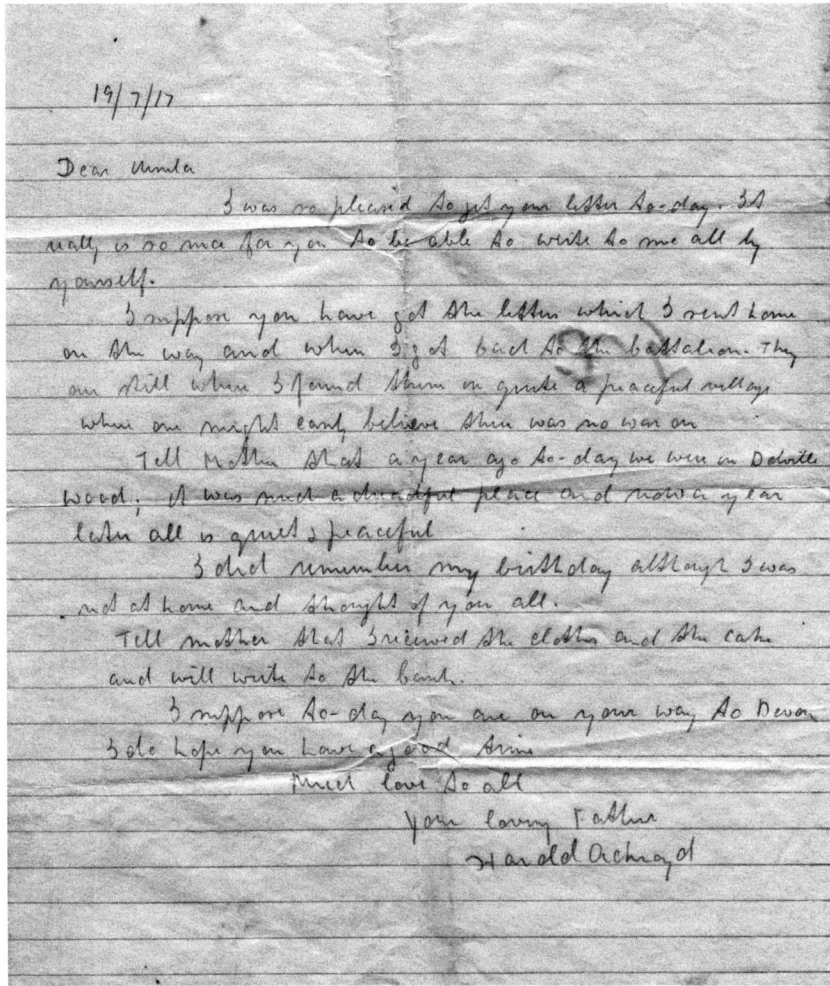

Last Letter Home – July 19th, 1917 (CMdeC)

Harold received this letter from his son Stephen, written by Mabel, when they were on holiday in Hope Cove, Devon enclosing a sprig of white heather which we still have preserved.

May Villa, Hope Cove, Nr Kingsbridge S Devon
August 1st 1917 (Our wedding day)
   Dear Daddy, We went to such a lovely place yesterday, high moors by the sea really lovely. We gathered heather and we are sending you some white heather for good luck, we got it ourselves. Our little bird is quite big now, he is a green finch and begins to twitter.
   With love and kisses from us all from Stephen

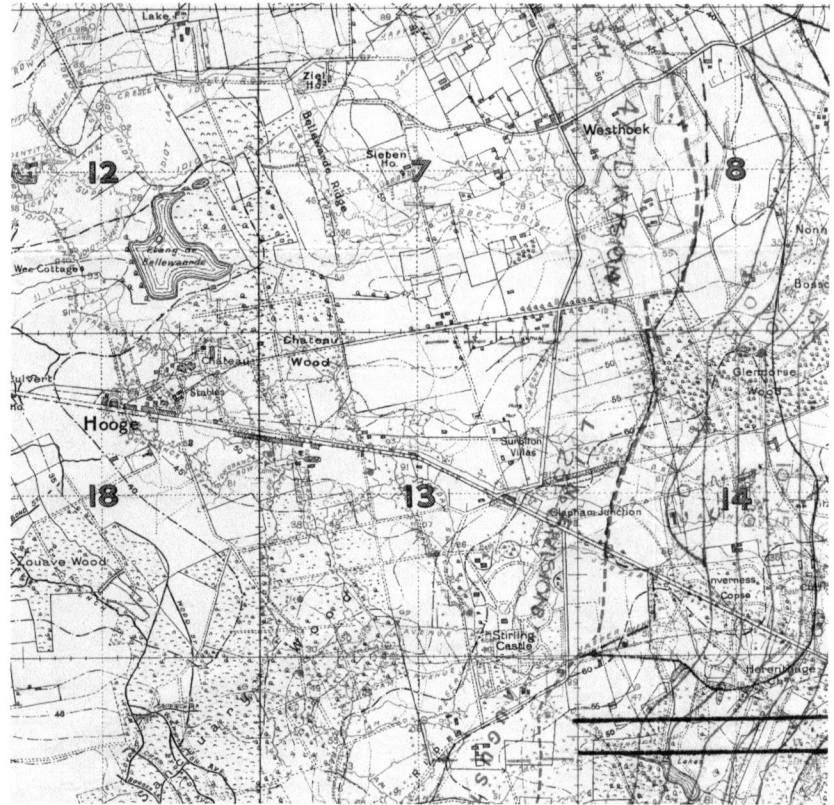

Trench map showing Glencorse Wood, Chateau Wood and Hooge in 1917

DISASTER

"The role of the 18th Division on the 31st July was to leap-frog the 30th Division after that Division had taken what became known as the black line. Deep behind enemy territory and seven hundred yards behind Glencorse Wood (the immediate objective) lay Polygon Wood which was to be the 18th Division's final objective. The High Command's plan was to strike with the 5th Army between Zillebeke and Zandvoorde Roads and Boesinghe on a front of seven and a half miles in length." (19)

"By a tragic mistake the 30th Divisional Infantry wheeled to their left and assaulted Chateau Wood instead of Glencorse Wood. The misleading information that Glencorse Wood was in our hands, caused the 53rd Brigade to plunge into a fatal gap. For the rest of the 31 July the 53rd Brigade was fighting against a fully-prepared enemy for the ground which the 30th Division should have taken. This fateful error caused the offensive in Glencorse Wood to be held up for several days." (20)

Captain Harold Ackroyd VC, MC, MD, RAMC (1877-1917)

"For the 6th Royal Berks the sticky, shell-broken slope from Sanctuary Wood to the Menin Road had to be carried. Then the road itself had to be secured before a chain of pill-boxes between the road and Glencorse Wood. Headway was gained dearly, a few yards at a time. The method was by sharp rushes from shell-hole to shell-hole under cover of our Lewis Guns. Before 10 o'clock the 6th Royal Berks, on the left of the Suffolk's, had taken Jargon Switch and the cross-roads north-west of Glencorse Wood; touch had been made with the 2nd Lincolns; the Surbiton Villas' line had been consolidated, with a support line in shell-holes; and Battalion Headquarters were established in the Menin Road tunnel." (21)

"And in all that hellish turmoil, there had been one quiet figure, most heroic, most wonderful of all. Doctor Ackroyd, the 6th Berks Medical Officer, rose to the supreme heights that day. He seemed to be everywhere; he tended and bandaged scores of men, for to him fell the rush of cases round Clapham Junction and towards Hooge. No wounded man was treated hurriedly or unskillfully. Ackroyd worked as stoically as if he were in the quiet of an operating theatre. Complete absorption in his work was probably his secret. When it was all over there were twenty-three separate recommendations of his name for the Victoria Cross. Some of the recommendations came from units of the 8th Division. Ackroyd's own battalion, the 6th Royal Berks, were accustomed to the bravery always shown by this middle-aged man of science – will the 53rd Brigade ever forget his glorious labours in Delville Wood?- and they did not ask for a Victoria Cross to be awarded him. Doctor Ackroyd went to war from the Downing College research laboratory at Cambridge. He was an absent-minded man. By a coincidence, one stretcher-bearer in the Division had been for years a laboratory attendant under Ackroyd at Downing. In France Ackroyd did not recognize him until the man said who he was. It was said that Ackroyd could tell a malingerer by instinct. He did not suffer weaklings patiently. In the training camps in England he was not popular. But out at the front his great qualities made him understood. After Delville Wood his nerves gave way. For a while blindness threatened him. That was why he took to wearing large shaded goggles. He came through 31st July without hurt, but was killed eleven days later in Jargon Trench, near Glencorse Wood. He died without knowing that the Victoria Cross had been awarded him. His name should never be forgotten." (22) Subsequent research shows that it was the Downing Street pharmacology laboratories, and not the College.

The Berkshires came out of the line on 1st August into reserve in heavy torrential rain. In the days that followed, recommendations for him to be awarded the Victoria Cross would have begun making their way up the system. So by the time they went back to the front Harold would indeed have been aware that his name had been put forward for the award.

> *"At 4.30 am on the 11th August, when the 8th Norfolk were relieving the Bedfordshire Regiment in the strong point in the south-west corner of Glencorse wood, it was rushed by a German counter-attack. The 6th Royal Berkshires were ordered to support the Norfolk Battalion in the recapture of the strong point. Captain Rochfort says that he was sent up to arrange covering fire for the attack. Two companies of the 8th Norfolk, at the bend of the Ypres-Memin Road, attacked a strong point, and at the same time "A" Company of the 6th Royal Berkshire, under Captain G.C. Hollis, bombed southwards from the west end of Glencorse Wood. The strong point was recovered though not without considerable losses. At 10.15 the 8th Norfolk, 10th Essex, and 6th Royal Berkshire were ordered to make an attack on the edge of Glencorse Wood, which had been gained by the 54th Brigade. But, in addition to the fact that the 8th Norfolk had lost heavily in the operations about the strong point, the 8th Suffolk did not turn up, and the attack was subsequently cancelled." (23)*

In a pause during repulsing an enemy attack on 11th August, Harold set off from his Advance Dressing Station to look for casualties behind the firing line. On this occasion he was not accompanied by his orderly, Private A Scriven, leaving him in charge of the Advanced Dressing Station.

According to Sergeant Maurice Butter, Harold had gone forward to tend to a wounded man lying in a crater actually in the front line.

> *"He reached the shell-hole, dressed the man, and as he got up to fetch the stretcher bearers a sniper shot him"*

Private Scriven wrote to Mabel on 16th September explaining in more detail what had happened. His first letter sent immediately after the action never arrived.

> *"He was visiting each company about 150 yards in front of us, to see whether there were any wounded to attend to and in so doing he had to go from one shell hole to another, and in so doing was shot through the head by a sniper. Immediately I heard the news I took a party of stretcher bearers, but on arrival found he was dead. There were six other poor fellows in the same shell hole who had met the same fate, it was a perfect death trap."*

The London Gazette of 6th September carried the announcement of the posthumous award of the Victoria Cross to Temporary Captain Harold Ackroyd, the citation read:

"For most conspicuous bravery. During recent operations Captain Ackroyd displayed the greatest gallantry and devotion to duty. Utterly regardless of danger, he worked continuously for many hours up and down and in front of the line tending the wounded and saving the lives of officers and men. In doing so he had to move across the open under heavy machine-gun, rifle and shell fire. On another occasion he went some way in front of our advanced line and brought in a wounded man under continuous sniping and machine-gun fire. His heroism was the means of saving many lives, and provided a magnificent example of courage, cheerfulness and determination to the fighting men in whose midst he was carrying out his splendid work. This gallant officer has since been killed in action"

INVESTITURE CEREMONY

Daily Telegraph Wed 26th September 1917

V.C.'s Publicly Bestowed by the King to Captain Ackroyd's Widow and little Son

On Wednesday last the King held an investiture at Buckingham Palace, at which his Majesty bestowed over 270 Naval, Military, and Red Cross decorations. There were 8 V.C.'s given, and a posthumous V.C. Most of the awards were conferred within the Palace, but the King had considerately arranged that the public should have an opportunity of seeing the bestowal of the Victoria Crosses. This part of the investiture took part in the Palace forecourt.

By his Majesty's special invitation, the two daring Italian aviators, who recently flew from Turin to London were among the privileged spectators. The whole length of the railings in front of the forecourt was thronged with sightseers, as also were the gallery and terraces of the Victoria Memorial opposite.

A guard of honour of the Grenadier Guards, with band and colours, was drawn up, and facing was a reserved space for wounded soldiers, naval and military Officers, Palace officials, and for the V.C. heroes, who occupied the first row of chairs.

In this party was a very pathetic little group, comprising the widow and little son of Captain Harold Ackroyd, R.A.M.C. (of "Brooklands",

Royston) upon whom both the V.C. and the Military Cross would have been conferred had he lived. The widow wore deep mourning, while the little boy was bareheaded, and was dressed in a white sailor suit.

Last in order to receive the Victoria Cross, says The Daily Telegraph, but certainly not the last in interest and human sympathy, came Mrs. Ackroyd and her little son. In their case the procedure was varied a little. The King advanced from the table to meet them, shook hands with both, spoke words of earnest sympathy, and made the bestowals without waiting for the reading of the record. It was a splendid record all the same.

The Victoria Cross his Majesty handed to the widow (who was keenly affected, but bravely restrained her emotion), and then he gave the Military Cross to the little boy. The youngster looked wide-eyed (Stephen was 5 1/2!) at the King, and appeared not to understand, whereupon his Majesty opened the case, showed him the decoration within, told him it was well won by his brave father, and patted his head. Throughout the ceremony was punctuated by the cheers of the on looking spectators.

The widow and the little boy had hardly resumed their places when the Royal Salute was repeated by the Guards, the band played the National Anthem, and the guard of honour marched away from the Palace.

The ceremony can be viewed on the IWM Photographic website under reference NTB 318-2. There are over 50 letters of condolence written to

Stephen and Mabel far left with VC recipients at Buckingham Palace for the Investiture, Wednesday 19th September, 1917 (IWM)

Captain Harold Ackroyd VC, MC, MD, RAMC (1877-1917)

Investiture at Buckingham Palace, Wednesday 19th September, 1917 – Mabel & Stephen receive the medals from King George V. (IWM)

Mabel, the most moving being that of Capt. J.N. Richardson whom was I believe the closest of Harold's comrades in the Battalion dated Aug 19th.

> *Dear Mrs. Ackroyd, I can't in the least way express my sorrow or offer you enough sympathy about your husband and our M.O. It's the biggest loss this battalion has ever suffered and its nothing more or less than a tragedy for us all. As you have probably heard before he was the most fearless man imaginable and to see him in his cool way picking up wounded and sending them off was a sight no one can ever forget. The hottest shell fire never stopped him going to a wounded man and the men used to simply stare in wonderment at his bravery. In all fights he was worth a hundred men to us for morale's sake. Doubtless it will make you extremely proud of your gallant husband, but on the other hand his loss may be still harder to bear. Sympathy I know is of little value in such cases, but I am so very grieved for you and your little children, especially Ursula whom I seem to know in a sort of vague way. I remain, Sincerely Yours,*
>
> > *J.N. Richardson.*

Harold was buried in Birr Crossroads Cemetery, Zillebeke, near Ypres. His headstone, on the right of the entrance gate is one that reads "Believed to be buried".

POSTSCRIPT

Mabel Ackroyd came to Jersey after the Second World War with her daughter, Ursula and son in law, Guy Malet de Carteret (my grandfather). She died on the 17th April 1947 and is buried in St Ouen's churchyard, with Ursula.

On Mabel's death in 1947, Harold's medals were inherited first by his eldest son, Stephen, who died without issue in 1964. They were then inherited by Anthony his second son until his death in 1988 then by his son Christopher, an Orthopaedic surgeon in Bristol.

The Victoria Cross together with his Military Cross and campaign medals had been "on loan" to the RAMC since "The Victoria Cross Centenary Exhibition" in 1956 at Marlborough House. The exhibition was attended by Tony and his wife Pat Ackroyd. Christopher aged 14 remembers pushing his father in his wheel chair (Tony had contracted Polio in 1947 and was left paralysed below the waist) and meeting the DGAMS, Major-General Sir William Drummond.

I first saw a replica of Harold's Victoria Cross in the Victoria Cross room at the old RAMC Headquarters in Millbank, London in the early 1990's. When I was told by the then Regimental Secretary, Colonel (Rtd) Gordon Fagg that the original was never seen as it sat permanently in a bank vault at RBS, I informed my cousin Christopher and suggested that

Harold's grave stone (author)

114

Harold - Oil by J. Hicks – 1994 (CEA)

he take them back into his possession. In fact, Christopher did take his family to see the medals in November 1983 when Col. Bob Scott, Professor of Military Surgery, arranged for them to be taken out of the Vaults at Aldershot. After some delicate negotiations with the Army, the medals were presented to Christopher at a moving ceremony and luncheon at the RAMC headquarters Millbank in April 1994. The medals were presented by the then DGAMS, Major-General Sir Frederick Mayes. They hung in the waiting room of his Orthopaedic Clinic and then at his home in Clifton, Bristol under the portrait that he had commissioned of Harold by a former patient, Bristol artist Jerry Hicks.

Philip Malet de Carteret, Elizabeth Malet de Carteret, Rev Ray Jones, Edward (Ned) Malet de Carteret, Christopher Ackroyd on 11th August, 2007 by Harold's grave at Birr Cross Roads Cemetery, Ypres for the 90th Anniversary of Harold's death memorial service. (author)

In 2003, after much discussion within the family, Christopher finally decided to sell the Cross and medal set. They were sold privately through Spink to an anonymous purchaser after a "cloak and dagger" meeting. The total proceeds of £120,000 were to endow an annual scholarship at Gonville & Caius College, Cambridge. Christopher agreed with the then Master, Neil McKendrick, that the scholarship of £1000 per year for four years would be awarded to a student in their second year who had achieved excellence in the first year exams and had made outstanding contributions to the corporate life of the College. There would also be an annual memorial lecture by a distinguished medical scientist. The college has now elected 17 scholars and there have been 16 annual lectures. In 2018 the scholarship committee of Gonville and Caius decided in consultation with the family to make a change to the terms of the scholarship. The Cambridge clinical

Harold's medals (Christopher Ackroyd, & Lord Ashcroft Collection)

medical course would now take place entirely at Addenbrookes Hospital and all medical students would spend six years in Cambridge. It was therefore decided that the scholarship would be awarded at the end of the second year and would run for the remainder of the course until qualification. I was privileged to attend the lecture in March 2007, which was given by Sir John Walker, a Nobel Prize winner.

It eventually transpired in 2006 with the publication of 'Victoria Cross Heroes' that Lord Ashcroft had bought the medals and they are now on proud display with the rest of his collection at the Imperial War Museum in London in the Lord Ashcroft Gallery. This was opened by the Princess Royal on 10th November 2010 and lilies of the valley were presented to her by Miss Mia Pearlman, Harold's great-great granddaughter aged 6 years. I viewed them for the first time in November

Harold's Victoria Cross obverse (Christopher Ackroyd & Lord Ashcroft Collection)

2013. They sit in a grouping along with Harold's fellow RAMC medic, the double VC winner – Noel Chavasse.

I have often visited Harold's grave, starting in the mid 1990's initially touring several times with Flanders Tours, the then tour operator for the Western Front Association. They were lead by Lt. Col. (Rtd.) Graham Parker OBE. My penultimate visit was for a

Harold's death penny (Courtesy C E Ackroyd)

Memorial Plaque in St Georges Church, Ypres, 2008 (author)

Christopher Ackroyd and author at Southport War Memorial, 2008 (author)

Southport Memorial. New Memorial Stone 2013 (Rab Peck)

moving 90th Anniversary memorial service for Harold which I organised on Saturday 11th August 2007. It was led by Rev. Ray Jones of St. George`s Church, Ypres. The Last Post was played by three buglers from the Last Post Association including a member who has played at the Menin Gate for over 50 years - Antoine Verschoot, MBE.

I had driven to Ypres from Jersey with my late father, Philip. The trip saw a couple of firsts for him, he had never been a passenger in France after 40 years of driving on the continent nor had he ever travelled to France by Condor Ferries! We met there with Christopher Ackroyd and his wife Alexandra and her son Thomas Plant and his wife Angela. My sister Elizabeth drove up to join us on the Saturday morning from Dahn in Germany.

Inscription Room S9, Tree Court, Gonville & Caius College (CMdeC)

It was a glorious day and after the ceremony we drove to Glencorse Wood where Christopher Ackroyd nailed a memorial cross to a tree in Harold's memory.

On the 100th Anniversary, Christopher, Alex and Ned organised a large pilgrimage of over 30 family members from England, Jersey and Germany. The memorial service at the graveside on Friday 11th August 2017 was led by the Reverend Gillian Trinder the then vicar of St George's church, Ypres. Some of the great great grandchildren contributed to the service and Christopher gave a eulogy on Harold's life. The Last Post and the Reveille were sounded by Col. Michael Taylor, great grandson- in- law. The party then went to the field below Glencorse Wood where Harold fell and four of his great great grandsons planted a memorial plaque on the spot.

Harold's name appears on the following memorials:

1) Shrewsbury School – on the statue and in the chapel.
2) Gonville & Caius College, Cambridge – on the Chapel memorial board.
3) Gonville & Caius College, Cambridge – Memorial Plaque on mantelpiece in Room S9, Tree Court together with a replica set of the medals, which was occupied by Harold when up at Caius.
4) Royston War Memorial, Royston, Herts.
5) Road name "Ackroyd Close", Royston, Herts.
6) A blue plaque on his old residence "Brooklands" 46 Kneesworth Street, Royston, Herts. SG8 5AQ.
7) Southport War Memorial and new VC commemoration stone (2013)

8) Southport War memorial paving stone laid on 6th September 2017.
9) Guy's Hospital Memorial Arch.
10) The British Medical Association – House Memorial
11) The RAMC Officers Quarters, Camberley, Surrey – matt oil painting.
12) The RAMC Officers Quarters, Camberley, Surry. Board listing RAMC VC winners.
13) The Fort Beaufort Historical Museum, South Africa – copy of RAMC picture.
14) On Mabel and Ursula's gravestone, St Ouen's Churchyard, Jersey
15) Ackroyd Troop. RAMC Training Group. Keogh Barracks, Ash Vale, Aldershot. GU12 5RQ. July 1988.
16) Memorial Plaque in St George's Church, Ypres (since 2008)
17) Ackroyd Scholarship, Gonville and Caius College Cambridge (2004).
18) National Memorial Arboretum, Alrewas, Staffordshire.

Ursula by J. Hicks (author)

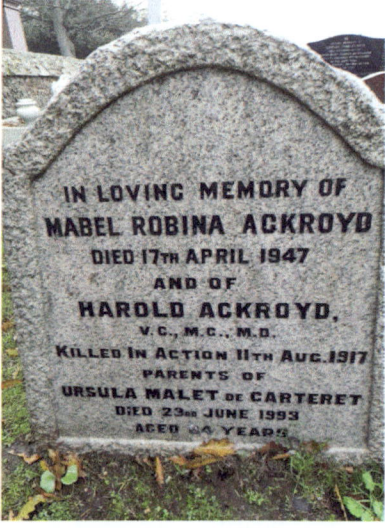

Mabel & Ursula's Gravestone, St Ouen's Churchyard, Jersey (author)

Captain Harold Ackroyd VC, MC, MD, RAMC (1877-1917)

Placing our memorial, Glencorse Wood.
(Courtesy CE Ackroyd)

Ned, Charlie, Liz,Bob Malet de Carteret,
11/8/2017 (Courtesy CE Ackroyd)

Group photo outside Ariane Hotel, Ypres (Courtesy CE Ackroyd)

References/Sources:

(1) Ackroyd H, On the presence of Allantoin in certain foods. 1911, Biochemical Journal, 5,400-406.

(2) Ackroyd H, On Purine metabolism of Rats. 1914, Biochemical Journal, 8; 434-437.

(3) Ackroyd H and Hopkins FG, Feeding experiments with deficiencies in the amino-acid supply: Arginine and Histidine as possible precursors of Purines. 1916, Biochemical Journal, 10; 551-576.

18th Division in The Great War. (Naval & Military Press from William Blackwood & Sons, 1922) by Capt G.H.F. Nichols

Notes: (4) p 16, (8) p 48, (10) p 71/2, (11) p 72, (12) p 72/3, (13) p 73, (14) p73/4, (15) p 74, (16) p 71/74, (17) p 194, (18) p 197/8, (19) p 202, (20) p 204, (21) p 205-207, (22) p 209/10

The Royal Berkshire Regiment, Vol 11 1914-18, by F. Loraine Petrie, OBE (Published 1925)

Ref: (5) p 253, (6) p 257, (7) p 254, (9) p 258, (23) p 279

War Diary – 6th Royal Berkshire Regiment (WO 95 3037)

Personal papers and letters: C.E. Ackroyd, MA, MB, B.Chir, FRCS, Clifton, Bristol

Personal papers and letters: C. G. Malet de Carteret, St.Ouen's Manor, Jersey.

CONDOLENCE LETTERS

In The Field
August 13th, 1917

Dear Mrs Ackroyd

I feel I must write and add my tribute to the memory of your dead husband.

I worked in Dixon's lab with him and then met him at Colchester nearly three years ago and ever since have been members of the same Division.

For most of the time I have been at Headquarters of the Division, a place that he did not hold in favour, but a place where one hears reports for many different sources, and, I know that there was no one in the Division better liked personally, or more admired for his bravery, throughout the whole Division.

Out of action we always considered him the most conscientious and efficient medical officer we had, and in action he simply never considered any personal risk at all. All of our medical officers are wonderfully brave, but your husband was quite in a class by himself.

We were all half sorry when he returned after getting blown up last July, for we knew that, if he came back, he would go on taking appalling risks, and that the end was almost a certainty, he of course knew this equally well, but he insisted upon returning to his beloved battalion. I only hope the country will pay his memory the only possible tribute, and grant the highest recognition for bravery. Of course he had earned every award there is for bravery a dozen times over.

I am afraid I have expressed myself very poorly, but I wanted to tell you how your husband was regarded by men outside his own battalion, who have watched and admired his work for more than two years of active service.

One of the special horrors of this war is that it is always the very best whom we lose.

Yours very sincerely

Alfred J. Clark (later Professor of Pharmacology, University College, London)

> *Irlam Rd Schools*
> *Bootle*
> *15/8/17*

Dear Mabel

I am sorry, so sorry I cannot tell you. Your loss and the bairn's loss is one beyond calculation and you know how my sympathy is with you. My own loss I need not tell you for you know that quite apart from his being my brother, there has gone nearly the only man about whom I cared in the world. If you get anything further in the way of details, let me know. The children won't really know their loss, but in years to come you and I if we are spared will see they understand that their father was one of the best, that they can look back on clean honest parentage with a life that has caused much joy to others and many good deeds hid under his bushel. The kid he was and everyone's memories of him will be of a very youthful energy for his age.

I had a letter from you today on business but have hardly looked at it. I believe you are in a position to get any money you may require for immediate necessities from a Bank. I shall have to consider business questions at once, but not tonight Mabel dear.

Your loving brother

Edward Ackroyd

344 Protection Co
Irlam Rd Schools
Bootle
17/8/17

Dear Mabel

I suppose you had an official wire and if so it is very sad but there is little doubt of its being true. Poor Mabel I don't really know how to write to you perhaps all the more because we understand one another and we both loved him so much that what is unspoken will still be understood. But if it can avail anything, write just what you think, just what you want" the sad mechanic exercise like dull narcotics numbing pain"

Little Mayarel wrote to me so sad and what must it be for your wee bairns.

I know two people who have offered to come to you, and either of them would be of help, but it is the bairns of his flesh and blood that must be your living memory. Presently I must see you. In the meantime, if you can, write me as fully as possible where all necessary papers are deposited and what you want at once. I have sent a short note to the Southport paper, but it was not worthy of the subject. I bare not the heart easily to the pen.

Your loving brother
Edward Ackroyd.

August 19th 1917

Dear Mrs Ackroyd

I have been trying for the last few days to write to say how very much I personally and the whole Battalion mourn the loss of your gallant husband. The work that he has done for this Battalion will never be forgotten and it is indeed a calamity that he should have lost his life as he did.

I looked upon your husband as the most gallant man I have ever met and previous to his death had recommended him for the highest honour a man can get.

Whether this coveted distinction will be conferred I cannot say but I can truthfully state that it was thoroughly well earned and I hope very much his services will be as fully recognised outside the Battalion as they were in it.

I do not wish to take up your time but I thought it might be some slight comfort to you in your loss to let you know how much we all regret his loss and honour his memory. He together with a brother officer lie in the cemetery at Ypres.

If there are any details I can supply I hope you will mention them
With sincere sympathy
Yours sincerely
B.G. Clay (Lt. Col 6th Royal Berks)

He left the Royal Berks to commanded 7th Battalion Guards Division, and was awarded the CMG and DSO. He died in 1937 aged 62.

Aug 20

My dear Mrs Ackroyd
I hope you will forgive me but I feel I must write to you and offer you my very deepest sympathy in your terrible loss.
Your husband was always such a good friend to us we were such great pals. His death to us was a terrible shock.
He was killed trying to help others who were wounded; and hundreds of men in this battalion and others owe their lives to him. For in every action he was always rescuing and tending men who had been hit. His death is one of the worst blows the battalion has ever had and there is not one of us officers or men who do not feel his loss most terribly.
Please do not trouble to answer this as I know how many letters you will be getting.
With my deepest sympathy
Yours sincerely
Harold Longhurst. (Lt.Col).

H.G.F. Longhurst was killed two months later in action at 6.30am on 12th October, 1917 at Battalion HQ

August 23rd
Dear Mrs Ackroyd
I hope you will accept my deep felt sympathy at your great loss by the death in action of your husband. I always looked on him as one of the best medical officers of the Division, both when his battalion was out at rest and when in action. He had a very high sense of his duty and never spared himself in looking after the welfare of the officers and men under his care. His high sense of duty led him to expose himself almost too much in action, but, it led to the admiration of all and to the greatest trust and confidence being reposed in him by the officers and men of his battalion.
He was one of the most popular men in this Division and I myself feel that I have lost a very great friend and one for whom I had unbounded

admiration. His death came as a great shock to me and I feel that we can never adequately replace him. It is impossible to express in a letter how much I feel for you and the children, and wish I could be of some use. With the very deepest sympathy,

Believe me, Very sincerely yours
J. Roe Colonel
A.D.M.S. – Division

"6" Company 11th Battn ? DC
Irlam Road Barracks, Bootle
28/8/17

Dear Mabel

These letters are proud reading. If God willed that he should be one of the awful sacrifices of this war, it is something that his last two years leave much a record of nobility. You and I knew without being told that there would be no shrinking from danger or from work. The double result is that he saved the lives of others and that the battalion M.O. enormously aided the military officers in producing an efficient battalion in morale and discipline.

So, if it is we grieve Mabel just the same. I have only a small envelope here so will return the letters later. I am writing at the Battalion Headquarters where I am on duty for the day which mostly means doing little but waste time, a game, I don't like as there is plenty to do.

Don't worry about the London City & Midland Bank book, it will do when you return to Royston as I can get any figure I want from the Bank itself. I got the Key and have a note from the Bank that they have got the box. There will have to be a general clearing up of his pay account at Holts. I note as to the Exchequer Bond Certificates, but I thought it had all been converted to 5% War Loan.

If there is any high honour coming to Harold, the person who should receive it dear Mabel is yourself and the boy.

I am afraid that it is impossible to prevent the gross amount of an estate getting into the papers. You see it is public property for anyone who searches at Somerset House and that I how the papers get their information. People constantly want to keep it out and I know that they are not successful. I will go down to Southport in a day or two and get things moving if I can.

I hope you are having better weather than we are, as the more you are out of doors with the children the better.

Your loving brother
Edward Ackroyd

Captain Harold Ackroyd VC, MC, MD, RAMC (1877-1917)

2nd Sept, 1917

My dear Mrs Ackroyd

Pressure of work has prevented me from writing sooner to express to you my sincere sympathy in the sad loss which you have sustained through the death of your gallant husband.

I fear that I can say little which will be of real comfort to you and I can only offer you my heartfelt condolences. He was one of the most gallant and true-hearted gentlemen that I have ever met. He was absolutely fearless and his unselfish devotion to duty was an example to us all. Every officer and man in the Brigade, who knew him, had the highest admiration for him.

If you could only have heard the way the officers and men of the 6th Royal Berkshire Regiment spoke about him you would feel doubly proud. He was recommended for the Victoria Cross for his gallantry and devotion to duty and I sincerely hope it will be awarded to him. He deserved it if any man ever did.

I have no doubt that you have heard particulars of his death from the Royal Berkshire Regiment. If I cam be of any service to you please let me know. My address is – Headquarters, 53rd Infantry Brigade, B.E.F.

We all mourn the loss of a most gallant comrade.

With kind sympathy

Yours sincerely

H.W. Higginson

(Brig. Gen) Later Major-General Harold H Higginson, CB, DSO and Bar commanding the 12th Division. He died in 1954 aged 80.

September 8th, 1917

Dear Mrs Ackroyd

Not receiving an answer to my letter I wrote you on the 15th August I am beginning to wonder if you received the letter of condolence I sent you on that date.

I was Captain Ackroyd's servant and was with him when he was sniped through he head. He never uttered a word and death was instantaneous, so I am sure he never suffered. I was gratified to read in the "Daily Mail" that he was awarded the V.C. which he richly deserved in Delville Wood, how we all would have liked to have seen him live to have worn the honour. He was the most popular officer in the battalion, and loved by all ranks, his place can never be refilled.

I have sent off his kit to Cox & Co, and all the personal effects by registered post also to Cox & Co. The sovereign purse with a sovereign in, I gave to our adjutant to post while on leave, to you at Royston.

Will you excuse me if I ask you a favour, and that is, could you kindly let me have a photograph of him, I feel certain you will not deny me that favour, he was so kind to me and treated me more as a friend than a master.

Again I send my sincerest condolences in the great loss you have sustained.

Trusting you will grant me my wish and to receive all the effects safely,

Believe me
Yours very sincerely
Scriven
Private A. Scriven
Headquarters
6th R.B.R.
B.E.F.

P.S. I trust I have done the right thing in cutting his buttons and badges off. These are in the registered parcel.

September 16th, 1917

Dear Mrs Ackroyd

Many thanks for your letter of the 13th and pleased you have received my second letter, the whereabouts of my first remains a mystery. I am afraid I could not tell you the contents of my first one, as I wrote it immediately we came out of action and one's nerves were in a very bad state owing to us all having such a rough time, but I know it was a very few lines.

We lost our Orderly Corporal the day before the action, therefore I was acting as such in charge of the Advanced Dressing Station, otherwise I would have been with the Captain.

He was visiting each company about 150 yards in front of us, to see whether there were any wounded to attend to and in so doing he had to go from one shell hole to another, and in so doing was shot through the head by a sniper. Immediately I heard the news I took a party of stretcher bearers, but on arrival found him dead. There were six other poor fellows in the same shell-hole who had met the same fate, it was a perfect death trap.

Thank you very much for your kindness in sending me a photograph. I think I would like an enlargement from a snapshot as the "Mirror" is hardly good enough of him.

I do trust you will receive his kit and effects safely and anxiously awaiting the photograph which I will send home for framing.

Yours sincerely

A. Scriven

September 20th, 1917

My Dear Mrs Ackroyd

It was with the very greatest pleasure that I read the announcement in the London Gazette of the award of the Victoria Cross to your gallant husband though one's pleasure was tempered with sadness at the thought that he is no longer with us and that he did not survive to wear the highest honour which a soldier can gain. It will be of some slight consolation to you in your sorrow and I know how proud you must feel.

We all miss our gallant comrade sadly but his memory will remain and he has inscribed his name on the immortal roll of V.C. heroes.

With kind regards

Yours sincerely

H.W. Higginson

October 12th, 1917

Mrs Ackroyd

Dear Madam

Thank you so much for your kind letter of 2nd also the photograph of Capt. Ackroyd which I have forwarded home to be framed and taken care of till I return. It's a very good photo and am very pleased with it but as you say it is a pity it is not clearer.

The Battalion attacked this morning and I am sorry to just learn that our action that Major Longhurst has been killed and Captain Rochfort (the Adjutant) has been wounded and I am afraid the rank & file have suffered heavily.

I cannot understand why you have not received the personal effects and Sovereign Purse, but I will immediately the battalion come out of action, will enquire through the proper channels and let you know further about them.

? went on leave about 3 weeks ago and has not returned, nor has there been any communication from him explaining his absence.

My address is below.

I do hope you are recovering from the shock caused through your irreplaceable loss.

Closing with the kindest regards to your children and to yourself.
Believe me,
Yours very sincerely
A Scriven
Mrs Scriven
27 Ingleby Road
Holloway. N7

27/12/17

Dear Mabel

As I said in my note written earlier in the day, it all centres around the word "Belief". You believe in the hereafter; it may be difficult to quite put your reasons on paper, but your belief is there. Not laughable but as tangible as love that you know for true. Others find "Belief" hard, wanting the tangible. Their standard of belief is such as their temperament, their studies, their education and environment enable them to afford. In many cases they have a far larger proportion of belief that they liken themselves would allow and when that is so quality in the belief is almost certain to be superficial.

I hardly think the writer at the end of the book gives sufficient weight to the evidences in action of the faith of men who die in battle where outward profession has been meagre.

Personally I feel large numbers of our dead have a greater grip on the Hereafter than those following their customary indifference in civil life. You and I will be loathe to abandon that hope of seeing husband and brother again.

Edward Ackroyd

Midshipman John Malet Armstrong (1900-1988)

John Malet Armstrong (Jock) was born on 5th January, 1900 at Elizabeth Bay, Sydney. He was the younger child and only son of William George Armstrong, a doctor (the 1st Director of Medical Services for New South Wales) and Elizabeth Jane nee Garnsey.

He was educated at Sydney Grammar School and All Saints College, Bathurst. In 1914 he entered the Royal Naval Australian College, Osborne House, Geelong, Victoria. The college was then relocated to Jervis Bay, Federal Capital Territory in February 1915. The first two years intakes joined the college, Jock in the second year at Geelong. A natural leader and sportsman, he became a chief cadet captain and received colours for rugby and swimming before he graduated in 1917.

His great grandparents were:

Jock in Uniform, date unknown (National Library of Australia)

Jock in Uniform in Garden, date unknown (National Library of Australia)

Francis Wheeler Armstrong (1779-1868) was born in Ireland, but moved to Jersey and bought St Peters House, in about 1820. He died on 15th April 1868 and was living at No 3 Almorah Crescent. Francis fought in all the major battles of the Peninsula War as a

HMAS Creswell, formerly RANC Jervis Bay (Google)

Francis Wheeler Armstrong (C MdeC)

Esther Armstrong (nee de Quetteville) (CMdeC)

Lieutenant in the 48th Regiment of Foot (Northamptonshire Regiment) from 1809-1814.

He married in 1819 in Grouville, Esther Francoise de Quetteville (1796 – 31st August 1865). They are buried together in Green Street Cemetery,

St' Helier, where you can see a new gravestone erected by Jock's eldest son David, within the past 5 years.

Jock's grandfather was Commander Richard Ramsay Armstrong RN (1833-1910) who was born on 28th February, 1833 in Jersey and died in Perth, Australia. He and his elder brother Robert both fought in the Crimea War and Richard was unlucky not to win a Victoria Cross at the taking of the Redan at Sevastopol. He married his cousin Eliza Suzanna Malet of St Helier on 20th August, 1857. She is related to the Mallet family of La Malletiere (Les Pres Manor) in Grouville (My family).

Commander Richard Ramsay Armstrong, RN

They produced Jock's father, William George, and his Aunt, Amy Anne Frances Armstrong (1865-1950) She married her second cousin, my great-grandfather Jurat Reginald Malet de Carteret (1865-1935) of St Ouen's Manor Jersey.

Reginald and Amy were married on 21st December, 1895 in Sydney, Australia, where my great-uncle Philip Reginald Malet de Carteret was born in 1898. My grandfather, Guy was born in 1901 and my great-aunt Ella Marie (Ellie or Elley) who was the eldest had been born in 1896. These family members feature heavily in Jock's letters home.

Jock therefore grew up with his cousin Midshipman Philip Malet de Carteret for the first six years of their lives or so.

Jock was appointed Midshipman on 1st January 1918, and he joined the latest battlecruiser HMAS Australia in April at Scapa Flow, Orkney.

HMAS Australia was a new battlecruiser and sister ship to HMS New Zealand. The ship had been launched in 1911 and commissioned in 1913. She was armed with 8x 12 inch guns and 16x 4 inch guns. Australia was capable of 25 knots. She commenced the War by trying to find and destroy the German East Asia Squadron. This sadly was not achieved. She only fired her guns twice in anger. Once at a German merchant ship in January 1915 and secondly at a suspected U Boat in December 1917. The ship missed the Battle of Jutland because she was being repaired after a collision with her sister ship HMS New Zealand a month before the battle.

Jock embarked for England from Melbourne, Australia on the SS Beltana – redesignated HMAT Beltana., she was the second of five 11,000 ton twin

HMAS Australia
(IWM – SP 1794)

Col EC Malet de Carteret
Reginald, Guy, Amy, Ellie,
Elizabeth, Enid, Jock.
Old Front Door,
St Ouen's Manor c. 1907
(CMdeC)

Officers of HMAS Australia. Jock is front row 3rd from the right
(National Library of Australia)

screw steamers built specifically for P&O by Caird & Co, Greenock, in 1912. The ship was 529 foot long and had a draught of 31 foot. She was capable of 14 knots. There was accommodation for up to 350 3rd class passengers and room for an extra 750 in the hold which could be removed to make way for cargo. The 'Beltana' carried a crew of 260.

HMAT Beltana (Google)

Here below are Jock's letters which I have lightly edited, some of his writing is difficult to read and some names are equally difficult to decipher. They normally took about two months to reach his parents in Sydney.

JOCK'S LETTERS HOME

Friday Evening 18th January, 1918

Train from ? to town

Dear Dad

We had a very good trip down and got plenty of sleep. Nell Joake and Mr Stapelton met us at Moss Vale and gave us coffee etc. arrived Melbourne good time and went to Williamstown. Reported, received £4 and then went on board "Beltana", have cabins, leaving tomorrow about 10. Going to town for a meal. Excuse the above writing but I did it in the train and am finishing at a restaurant. I am in a cabin with Dash who is a nice docile sort. Waller gets his medal tomorrow and as the "Beltana" leaves at 10 am we have to follow in the "Protector" or "Countess of Hopetown" and be put on board again.

Am having our last feed in Auckland. JM Armstrong

At Sea
January 1918

Written from an Australian Port
But not posted until South African coast reached

Dear Dad

We have just been told that there will be a mail leaving the ship tomorrow so here is the news to date.

Mr Staleton, Nell Joake and two other girls met us at Moss Vale and gave us a royal welcome. Mr Stapleton had provided coffee and cakes and big bags of fruit for us to take with us. Everybody wished us the best of luck and we gave three cheers as we went out.

The journey down was very comfortable but it was a good thing we had reserved seats on the other side of the train as it was crowded. As soon as we got to Melbourne we made a bolt for the Williamstown train.

At Williamstown we were kept waiting some time and then paid £4 which means we get 5/9 a day instead of 5/-. After pay we embarked in the picket boat and were taken to the wharf alongside which the transport was lying. By the way although our letters are not opened by the censor we are not to put anything in them that should be censored or to give dates or the name of the ship or the port. However you know the name of the ship. We were kept waiting sometime on the wharf but about six o'clock we went on board and stowed our gear in our cabins. I share a small cabin with Dash. They are not very large cabins as she only carried 3rd class passengers before the war but they are much better than no cabin at all.

Everybody went ashore for dinner. I went to the Paris café with Jack Rayment and had a first class dinner as it was our last meal on land in Australia. After dinner we went to the Tivoly which was passable. Everyone had to be at the wharf by eleven pm as Mr Dix had our pass but as he did not turn up till 11.45 we had a nice long wait.

On Saturday morning at nine o'clock we embarked again in the Naval Depot's picket boat and were taken to the Depot. There the G.G. inspected us all, as well as the men from the depot, and presented Waller with his medal. Then we went on board again as the transport had not left the wharf. She got under way almost at once. There was a good crowd to see the munition workers off. We arrived at the heads about five o'clock and went through at once. Our quarters are very comfortable and we mess with A.I.F. officers. Our duties are very easy as yet. We take on a couple of hours duty on the bridge or in the Engine room each day. We have half an hours Gym before breakfast and half an hour's signals in the evening. However I think there is more work for us in the near future. The munition workers and bricklayers do not look a very choice lot and some are I.W.W. men I think, more than half are going home to munition work to see what they can get out of it. The ship is very heavily loaded and has a very valuable cargo of copper, wool and rabbits on board. So far we have not had any bad weather but there is a long swell at present to which she is pitching. However it has not affected me in the slightest and none of us midshipmen have been sick yet.

Love to all your loving son
JohnMArmstrong

At Sea , February 9th 1918
Dear Family

I wrote you a letter at an Australian Port but we only spent the night there and cleared out before day break so the mails were not taken ashore. We have to be our own censors so suffice it to say that we are going the same way as Enid went. Rumour has it that all letters posted on board will be held back till we arrive in England, so I am posting this ashore, however I think it will be censored by the postal people.

Continuing on from my last letter, we only stayed in port for the night and got away at daybreak and that and was the last we saw of Australia. There was considerable swell on outside and they had to put fiddles on the tables still none of us have missed any meals so far. Every evening we have a formal dinner and drink the Kings health in water.

The President of the mess is a Major Richardson. Half the military officers are Doctors or Dentists and are quite new to their duties. The rest are wounded men who are returning to France. We have two of the Old Contemptibles aboard. A Lieutenant of the Black Watch whose name is Campbell and a Captain Granville, who was also ADC to one of Australia's numerous Governors. There are about a dozen Military Officers in all, and a very decent lot they are too. A few of the soldiers on board are Anzacs and tell some rather good stories. The Padre who is a Colonel and an Anzac is especially good at spinning yarns. On Monday evening we darkened ship because of a rumour that a 22 knot raider was about. However we have not met the raider so far and still have to darken the ship every night. This means that until all lights are off the dead lights have to be kept closed and it makes the cabins very hot. After we first came on board all our cabins had fans in them but they were not connected so some of the electrical geniuses purloined the missing parts from their neighbour's fans and got their own going. When the others got to hear of this they bided their time and pinched the required parts back again. When the ships electrician came along to fix all the fans he finds half the parts missing and removed the fans. Now we have to replace all the missing parts when we get to port or lose our fans for the rest of the voyage.

On Wednesday we had sports for the whole ship and Midshipmen got most of the prizes. They had a tug-o-war which we won easily. The numbers pulling were arranged by weight so we got ten men to every other teams eight. At night there was a bridge tournament. I went in for it and drew a sergeant major for my partner. We got right up to the finals but there our luck deserted us and our opponents won. Up to the finals we had had nothing but good cards all through and no one had scored below the line against us.

On Thursday morning we did gun drill at the old 6"we have aboard. She is a very old make and it required very good shooting to register anything like a hit. They would not allow us to do any shooting as they are only allowed five rounds for practice a month.

As Thursday was the last of the month the Gunlayer in charge of the gun fired his five rounds in the afternoon. I managed to get a very good view of the firing from the gun platform itself.

Mr Dix wanted me to get him a photo of the gun firing, unfortunately I forgot to turn the film on and took another on top of it. The Gunlayer scored three hits out of five which was quite good considering the age of the gun and the motion of the stern which is a figure of eight. The target was a cask which had been heaved overboard. The noise of the discharge was deafening from my position and I was half deaf all the evening. Once a week we have boat drill. There are three Midshipmen to every boat and we are in charge until a ships officer comes on board. There are about thirty munition workers in my boat and only two of us Midshipmen. The other Casey by name was ill when we left Melbourne and is following later on. The first time we had drill the munition workers took their own time but yesterday they were at their boats with lifebelts on in less than four minutes.

The ships officers are a very decent lot and help us as much as they can. With not having very much work to do, one hour on the bridge, one hour in the engine room and half an hour gym in the morning. Most of us take the practice of taking sights at 8 AM. I am getting quite expert and can get the ships position to a mile if she is not rolling too much.

There is not very much to do in the engine room as there is never anyone down there to explain things to us. For the rest of our time we do just about what we like which gets rather monotonous still we manage to spend the time somehow. Cards are in great demand and have learnt a lot about bridge.

Every second evening there is a concert or a card tournament or something like that. We all read a lot and there is a Y.M.C.A. library on board there is no shortage of books. It is just sixteen days since we last saw land and we expect to sight it in an hour or two. So far we have not met a single ship but we had wireless news all the time. I have eaten the cake mother packed for me and enjoyed it very much. We are able to get out our chests about once a week so stowed all my extra gear away. I found greatly to my surprise that my other two white tunics fitted me much better than the ones I took home.

I have taken a couple of films which turned out very well only I forgot to bring ordinary developer with me for prints so will not be able to send you any yet. By the way would you mind sending me a snapshot of Dad as I forgot to bring mine with me.

Land has just been sighted and I am off to have a look at it so good bye for the present.

Your affectionate son
JohnM Armstrong

At Sea
Posted in Portsmouth 2nd March 18

Received Sydney
8th May 18
Dear Mother
We stopped at Freetown for five days waiting for another ship to make up the convoy.

The harbour is realy an open roadsted with a big boom and mines across the seaward side. We went ashore almost every day but there was not much to see. Natives everywhere, in fact I think there are only about a hundred whites other than the English soldiers. When we arrived the harbour was full of ships. HMS "Bachante", a merchant cruiser and two big convoys in all about thirty ships. The battleship "Africa" came in while we were there. As soon as you get ashore you are mobbed by blacks trying to sell you something however they soon give it up. The town is on low lying ground at the foot of fairly high hills. The only hill in the town itself has the English barracks and the Governors house on it and a few English houses. We spent a lot of our time at the garrison club house and at the swimming baths which belong to the officers of the garrison. They are right on top of the hill and of fresh water. The baths can't be used in the dry season as there is not enough water for them. However we enjoyed them very much. Bargaining at the native shops was exciting especially as you were generally taken down. The Indian shops were better but you could never get the price down more than a couple of bob. The usual thing with the Indians was to toss for it. The shopkeeper would ask 10/- for something, you would say 6/- and he would want to toss for 7/- or 13/-. I lost once and did not try again. The blacks usually asked either 5/-, 10/-, 15/- for what ever they wanted to sell and you could be fairly sure that even if you paid 1/- to 22/6 for it you would be taken in. There is a small railway from the town to a place called Hill Top where all the English officers live. I went up there one day with Jack Rayment but there was not much to see. And all we had to do was eat fruit. We left Freetown on a Tuesday evening in company with six other ships, a slow convoy – and the "Armadale Castle" merchant cruiser is our escort. The Armadale got to work right away and generally tied the convoy up in knots making sarcastic remarks the while. I was on the bridge on duty and our skipper got quite wild. He had good reason to. Our signalman was lent us by the Armadale and is only a R.N.R. man and he tied up his own flags. The flags are not handy as they are in a naval ship but once off the halliards there is no time to put them away and they lie around all over the place. We do two hours a day on the gun and two hours on the bridge. By this time we are quite good at the Merchant code and relieve the signalman sometimes. It is getting very cold now at nights and the woollen gear you made me is very comforting, especially when I get gun duty from 2 to 4 AM. We are the loading numbers at the gun in case of action until the arrival of the remainder of the gun crew and then we have to spot the fall of the shots. There are always two of the gun crew on duty with us and the others sleep near by. On the bridge we keep a lookout and help the signalman. Ever since Freetown except when there is no moon at night we have been zig-zagging. Each ship zigzags in Greenwich time and with a stop watch to ensure they all turn together, all the same the Armadale is always shaking someone up for being out of station. Every ship is darkened at night and no one is allowed to smoke on deck. During the tropics it was very annoying not to be able to open our cabin ports but it is not so bad now although rather stuffy. We embarked some more soldiers at Freetown and several officers returning to England after a long spell on the frontiers. Most of the officers who have just come from Freetown and German East have been down with malaria. They say the cold weather brings it out. One of the officers from German East showed us some photos taken there which were very interesting. There were some of the "Konningsburg" before and after she was captured and any number of other German ships which had been captured. We put in most of our spare time playing hockey with walking sticks, or deck tennis which consists of chucking a large heavy leather ball about, or anything else to keep you warm. Bridge is played by nearly everyone in the evenings. The munition workers have been behaving better than they did at first and when ever there is a boat parade they run as if several devils were after them. I don't know w hat would happen if there was a parade at night. I think they would rush the boats. One of them shot himself in the leg about three days ago but I think he is mad as every time he was asked how it happened he gave a different answer. One of the Australian officers developed measles today, I hope we shall not be quarantined.

At six o'clock this morning our destroyer escort met us. One of them has a captive balloon for the spying out of submarines. At three this afternoon two of the convoy left us for Liverpool and the Armadale also left us. We just got orders to proceed direct to London but I think the Captain wirelessed for permission to land the passengers troops etc at Devonport as he does not wish to go up the channel with a lot of people on board. Goodness only knows what we shall do but I think we will proceed to Portsmouth to kit up. I do hope I will be able to see Enid. I got my No 1 uniform pressed and cleaned the other day. A munition worker who had been a cleaner before he joined up did it for the modest sum of 4/- and rather well too.

It is rather funny to hear them talking. They are not nearly so cocky as they used to be and there are rumours that some of them that are fit will be conscripted.

Well goodbye for the present, we hope to get in within the next three days even if we have to go to London.

Your most affectionate son
JohnMArmstrong

Grand Hotel Leicester
March 24th 1918

Received 1.6.18
Dear Dad

We arrived safely at London on Tuesday afternoon after a very uneventful trip up the channel. Two ships of the convoy left us off Lands End or there abouts to go to Liverpool and three more bound for Southampton. The "Beltana" and the "Ormeston"? were left to do the trip to London escorted by two destroyers and another which had the observation balloon. The only excitement was when we got lost off Dover. The entrance to the enclosed area is near Dover and it is only about two hundred yards wide it is rather hard to find. Also it is dangerous to go wandering round as you never know when you may strike a mine. However the destroyers soon found the passage and on we went. Once inside you are at once surrounded by shipping of all sorts and sizes from Battleships to Thames Barges while half an hour before you were all alone except for the escort. We took a pilot on board at the entrance and proceeded in single file to Tilbury, where we came to our anchor. A commander from Australia House came on board and told us we were to get ashore at once and entrain for Devonport. This was easier said than done as the crew finding themselves in Port refused to do Stevedores work ie shift our chests out of the hold, unless they got Stevedores pay. The Company was not willing to do this so we stayed on board that night. Next morning we were supposed to get up to the Albert Docks only a heavy fog made it impossible to move until the tide was too low so there we stayed. After Dinner, a large ferry came alongside and the crew very kindly consented to get our chests up and away we went to Tilbury wharf. There we got a train to Princes Station. After a wait of an hour big vans arrived for our gear and we got a tube for Waterloo. We just got there in time to get the seven o'clock train to Portsmouth where it seemed we had been going from the first. At Portsmouth we went to the "Terrible" a depot ship where we are going to stay and kit up. Who do you think was the first person we saw on the "Terrible"? None other than Captain Morgan who was in charge of her. He welcomed us with open arms and ever since has done his best for us in every way possible. When he leaves the ship at night, he lives ashore, we are allowed to use his cabins. We sleep in a Dormitory and are members of the Wardroom Mess. As soon as I landed I began a telegraphic communication with Enid and got leave for the Week end. Early on Saturday morning I was hauled out of bed by a Telegram from her asking me to come up by the early train. So I dashed round got the Commander to sign all sorts of papers station tickets etc and finally arrived at Leicester about two in the afternoon. Enid was on the station to meet me looking fit and well as could be. That afternoon I was taken up to the Hospital and shown all over it and incidentally introduced to the fearsome personage the matron. It is an enormous place and you could quite easily lose your way at first. I stayed at the Grand Hotel for the night and began this letter. On Sunday afternoon Enid got leave and we went back to London.. We stayed at Berners Hotel and the first person we saw was Uncle Tancred looking very well. He took us out to Dinner but we were not able to see anything of him on Monday as he was very rushed. On Monday morning I saw the Manager of the Commercial Bank and fixed up about my money. I drew GBP 25 and put it to current account as it will be much handier. Then we went to see Uncle Tancred at Australia House but he was out so Enid left a note. We lunched at "Ye Old Cheddar Cheese" and saw where Dickens and Dr Johnson used to sit. In the afternoon we went to a matinee called Lilac Domino which was very good. We had dinner at the Rendezvous where Uncle Tancred had taken us the night before and the Enid caught the eight o'clock train back to Leicester. I got an early train back to Portsmouth next morning. We are being fitted out at "Gieves" who is the naval tailor of Portsmouth, you pay for it too. The Government is giving us one new uniform and a host of minor gear. I have ordered another uniform as Captain Morgan said we would want two. Mr Darley has been very good to me. He kept Enid informed as to when I would arrive and asked another Midshipman and me to dine with him the night after we arrived. He is at Whale Island and is taking a batch of Lieutenants through a six months gunnery course!!

I enjoyed the dinner very much although slightly overawed by sitting down to dinner surrounded by Captains and Commanders etc. The Wardroom at Whale Island is very fine and their collection of silver I believe is the best there is. Each batch of Lieutenants give something when they leave so they have got an enormous lot there. I also met a Dr Macintosh there who knows Uncle Tancred very well and who studied Public Health at the Sydney University under you.

By the way the Government is giving us telescopes and binoculars so we won't have to get either. Very nice ones they are too in very strong leather cases. When I got back to the "Terrible" I found that our appointments were ready for us. I am in the "Australia" with eleven others so her gunroom will be all Australian. I am very pleased to get in the "Australia" in a way as she may go out home if the War finishes soon. On the other hand she has been nicknamed the Neutral Flagship as she has not been in anything yet. Did you hear that Cunningham of the first lot of Midshipmen was drowned a short time ago. He was in a submarine which was rammed by one of our own ships, awful hard luck was it not. On Tuesday afternoon and Wednesday we went round seeing places. Wednesday morning we went over to Vernon which is the big torpedo school and in the afternoon wee were taken in a picket boat down to Cowes in the Isle of White and went over Osborne. The buildings are really only temporary but there is no white out there as at Jervis Bay. The grounds are magnificent and so is the College generally. The cadets only do one year there and then go to Dartmouth for two. We were shown round by a party of c.c's. Next morning we went to the submarine base and went over a couple of submarines guided by a very interesting Lieutenant. In the afternoon some of us went to Gieves again and were fitted. I bought some more shirts and a pair of shoes. Owing to the Easter holidays our uniform wont be ready for some time so were given Easter leave. I did not get enough to go over to Jersey, so I am spending it in London with Enid. She managed to get two days leave although owing to convoys arriving from the front she was very lucky to get it. On Saturday I went up to Leicester and we came down together in the evening. This morning we went out to Richmond and got a boat and spent a couple of hours on the river. Then we went to Hampton Court and looked over it. I am very glad I don't have to live in a place like it. Then we came back to town on a bus and went to Westminster Abbey but we were too early for the evening service and so back to the Ivanhoe Hotel where we are staying.

The rationing does not effect us very much. You cannot get meat without tickets in London and sugar is also hard to get. Of course the bread is all war bread but it is quite nice. On board ship we are not rationed at all we just have to be careful not to waste anything.

I don't know when I will join my ship but I think it will be towards the end of this week. Eleven other midshipmen are appointed to the Agincourt and five to the Canada, so we are going in lots of three instead of five.

Your loving son
John.MArmstrong

PS: I wrote to Uncle Rex but I have not heard anything from him yet. Uncle Tancred wished to be remembered to you and mother. Thanks very much for your letter and for mothers, they beat me over here by nearly a week.

HMAS "Australia"
April 9th, 1918

Received June 10th, 1918
Dear Dad

Here we are at last after many wanderings. We seem to have been on the way for weeks and really it is only three days. When I finished my last letter I was in London with Enid. The next morning we went first to St.Pancras then to Waterloo to leave our respective luggage and who should we meet but Major Parkinson. He was waiting at Waterloo for a troop train and was on his way to France having landed at Liverpool only two days before. Enid was very glad to see him and we wanted to carry him off with us but he had to leave quite soon. He brought over a lot of gear for Enid from the Sydney Red Cross which he had left with some friends down at Streatham Hill a suburb of London. As we were not able to see him off we went down to Streatham before lunch and got Enid's things. She had to borrow a suitcase to put them in and even then there were some left out. In the afternoon we went to Chu Chin Chow which we enjoyed very much, it was even more gorgeous than Bing Boys. Enid went off by a six o'clock train for Leicester and I caught one that evening for Portsmouth.

Next day the Port Admiral inspected us and was graciously pleased to give us advice. He was a very awesome person with three ½" stripes above his thick one. That afternoon we went aboard the "Victory" and were shown over her by a marine, really the change of a hundred and ten years in ship construction is somewhat striking. There is a battleship in dock quite close to the "Terrible" she is being blistered which is a protection against torpedoes and consists of a large blister of iron all round ship along the waterline. The air was hideous with the sound of pneumatic riveters and drills and the night was lit up with the oxyacetaline flares. On Friday we got our kit from Gieves and the uniforms are very good.

My word it was great to get into good uniform after our old ones. On Saturday morning we all left the "Terrible" and went up to London under the charge of a Commander Hudson. We spent the afternoon at a picture show and caught a naval train for Inverness in the evening. Our first orders had been for Edinburgh but at the train we got fresh ones for Thurso, in the far north. The journey was rather tiring but it was very pretty up in the Highlands. When we got to Inverness we midshipmen for the "Australia" were told that we had to go south again. We had to spend Sunday night at the Railway Hotel and came back to Edinburgh the next morning. Inverness is a very pretty town when you get out of it a bit but it was rather cold.

We got on board on Monday evening and went to the Gunroom at once. The Gunroom is very full there are thirty three in here and three subs left the day we arrived. Six of the old fourth year are next seniors to us and there are four RN snotties senior to them. There are three subs, an AP, two engineer subs and an RMR sub and five clerks. The RN snotties will be going up for their subs exam in three weeks time. Then we will have the RAN snotties as the seniors of the mess till September when they will go up for their exam and we will be the seniors of the mess although we wont be senior snotties until January next. We will most probably go for our subs exam in September twelve months. The sub of the mess is named MacGuiness and although no one has run up against him yet we hear we will be lucky if we don't. Jack Rayment and

I are in the quarterdeck division under a Lieutenant Miller. We are also in X Turret which is the after turret for action stations.

My post when at sea other than action stations is in a control hut of the after 4" battery. On Tuesday we were put on two hours notice which means that all leave is stopped but it is quite common to be on two hours notice for weeks without leaving port.

While being shown over X Turret I managed to drop a dummy ¼ charge on my foot and I have been lame since then however it is nearly all right now. On Thursday evening I was duty picket boat and did three trips in her. I enjoyed it very much but there was a strong wind blowing and my word but was cold. On coming back from my last trip the fleet (battle cruisers) broke into a mass of bunting and when we arrived we heard we were ordered to proceed to sea in two hours time. The orders were cancelled half an hour later. So we turned in. However we went to sea at midnight and I was called at 2 AM to do my watch in the 4" control. The ship had only just been painted and I managed to wipe off most of it on to myself before I finally found my station. It is a small iron hut above the after 4" platform which is a raised superstructure just forward of the after turret. There are two of them one either side of the superstructure. They are just boxes with a narrow window all round and numerous telephones and voice pipes. I keep a look out for submarines and pass on any orders from the fore control. I will continue later as I have to go to my station for two hours. Up at the station it was rather cold and very little to do so I was quite glad when it was over. The fleet steamed along in line ahead with destroyer screens and turned continually, it just seemed to be going nowhere. There was a fog and the second astern was barely visible. We got back to port in the evening and coaled ship as soon as possible. We only had four hundred tons to get in and we did it in very good time though I don't know the exact times. I was in the after hold of the coaler and had a shovel. My word we were dirty when we finished and very glad to turn in. I am very glad that your lumbago is all right again. I just got your letter while I got mothers two weeks ago. My word it is nice to get letters from Aussie Land. I got one from Nell Joake with a lot of snaps of last leave. We are all very happy so far and like the ship very much and I think we are very lucky to be on her.

Your affectionate son

JohnMArmstrong

By the way the others all went up north and I think we have the best of it down here as they say it is very cold there. Mr Dix is aboard the Australia and a draft arrives today from Australia which contains a lot of old school hands from the College.

Midshipman John Malet Armstrong (1900-1988)

HMAS Australia
April 28th 1918

Received 17th June, 1918
Dear Mother

We have just got a mail from Australia the second since we left, and everybody is busy reading their letters. We have been coaling all to day from eight oclock till three in the afternoon. We had seventeen hundred tons to get in, quite a respectable amount and the mail came in the middle of it. You should have seen us at lunch. Everyone coal black except where we had washed our hands and mouths sitting around the table munching cold meat and bread and butter and reading "Aussie" mail. I got two letters from Dad and one from you and one from Kath Gaden.

When we got back from our first convoy trip we took in 1000 tons of coal and went to sea again in the evening. While we were in port we got the papers giving the account of the Zebrugge stunt. From what I hear it was an extremely fine show one of those Nelson touches. There were some stokers there from the "Australia" but none were injured which pleased everyone very much. The thing must have been planned for some time as these men left the ship about two months ago. I suppose they were rehearsing the show. To continue, after coaling we put to sea and next day picked up a convoy. It was very calm all the time we were out, in fact both times we have been out it has been extraordinarily calm and fairly warm. With the outward convoy we sighted two submarines and our destroyers dropped depth charges on them but it is not known if they were successful. A depth charge is a sort of mine which is lowered from the destroying ship over the spot where the sub is thought to be and is then exploded. If the sub is within three or four hundred yards she is generally turned over and if any nearer she is sunk. You can hear a depth charge a very long way off, it sounds just like something hitting the ship a smart blow under water. After being out two days we dropped our convoy and picking up another returned to port to take in sixteen hundred tons. Each part of the ship takes the hold of the collier which corresponds to its name. There are four holds QD (?) have the after hold and so on. Our hold was full to the brim and we cleaned it right out. We averaged about 220 tons per hour I think not counting stops for breakfast and lunch.

I am going to turn in now I am abominally tired.

Monday: As we coaled yesterday they excused us doing Gym this morning, as a result, everybody slept in and the Commander happened along. We have to fall in every morning and be reported correct to him by six am, which I suppose is good for us, but very uncomfortable at the time. However we are treated very well and in fact I think we escape many things which RN junior snotties have to put up with, and which we would not escape in any ship other than the "Australia"

While at sea I keep watch in the Starboard after 4" control hut. Ordinarily there are four of us doing duty there but this last trip to sea Palmer went sick with a bad cold and there were only three of us to do the duty which meant four hours on and eight off instead of two on and four off which is quite a different thing. You are on the lookout all the time and found there is no room for movement so four hours is rather long. However Palmer is now happily recovered and all is well again. Morgan who is the Admiral's doggie is down with Pneumonia but he is passed the critical stage and enjoying the prospect of two weeks in hospital with two weeks sick leave to follow. He was very bad I hear during the first two days but at present is lying in state in the Admiral's spare cabin. By the way the Admiral's name is Levison, the Captain's is Backhouse and the Commander's is Maxwell. We also carry a Commander N and a Commander E, to say nothing of a fleet Pay and a fleet surgeon, so we are well provided with brass hats. To day we have been getting in some new projectiles in place of a batch of Lydite which is pronounced dangerous.

When we are at sea we do no other work besides our watch stations so we have an easier time than in harbour. Of course we are continually practising action stations and having dummy runs at Control, but otherwise we do so very little work. The only thing is coaling when we get to port again and is rather awful.

The RN snots had the first day of their exam for subs to day. It lasts for three weeks and half is oral. It seems funny them going for their subs exams, I am older than the three of them and two are still under eighteen and are not allowed to smoke yet. Three of the Australian snotties senior to us are in destroyers for a three week course. One of them was in a sweep off the Skagerrak last week and helped sink a lot of trawlers. I hope you had a good holiday up at Exeter. I can imagine that it must have been delightful at this time of the year. Did dad go for a cruise with Mr Busby? I envy him if he did.

Dad tells me that Pat goes into the water without any fuss now, he must have progressed very much. I'm glad he defended his biscuit against the bulldog it shows there is some gut in him. Did you find any more snakes in the garden at Exeter? It is getting comparatively warm here now but not like Australian warmth

Here's to the next mail
Your affectionate son
JohnMArmstrong

PS: I can't send you any photos as cameras are kept very dark or they have to be given in

We are not permitted to give the name of our base although our letters are not censored but it is enough to say that on a make and mend afternoon we can get up to Edinburgh.

HMAS Australia
May 19th 1918

Received 9th July, 1918

Dear Dad

Many thanks for your letter dated March 31st and for the photo of yourself. It is a very good one in fact I think it is the best I have seen of you. It seems rather funny that you should have been wearing whites even at the end of March.

It has been quite warm for the last week and yesterday and today have been regular Australian days, a light breeze blowing and quite hot in the sun. Last night I slept without any blankets. For a wonder too there has been no rain for over a week.

There is nothing much doing at present. We are still in harbour and have only been out once last week. Then it was to do a night firing. They had a sub-callibre run with the big guns in the afternoon and in the evening it was the 4". By the way when I say evening I mean nearly midnight as it does not get dark here till after ten o'clock.

The Commander has decided that we are not getting enough work so we will do more watches and more picket boat work, however it makes little difference we can still get ashore four afternoons in every week if we want to. I went up to Dunfermline this afternoon. It is a middling town a little nearer although in the opposite direction to Edinburgh. It is not much of a place anyhow not on a Sunday. We could not get any afternoon tea, quite a necessary feature of any expedition ashore, and the place was overrun with sailors and mostly Yankie at that.

I met some of my friends from the Canada and Frank McMahon from the Agincourt. They don't appear to be having such a pleasant time in their Gunroom as we do. I also met Guy Windeyer. He was flying around and seemed to be enjoying himself. He is in the "Thunderer" He is not very tall but is quite hefty and says he has taken up boxing. His seniority dates about four months ahead of mine but I think we catch up that or most of it when we go for our subs exam. He said that he was getting very homesick and tired of England. The three RN snots have finished their exams although they do not know if they have passed yet they are to put up their stripes as the Commander wants some more watch keepers. It seems funny one of them is still a kid in his ways and only one is over eighteen. They are the one fly in the ointment in the mess to us. They of course cannot make us fag for them but they have a nice habit of carrying their little troubles to the sub of the mess who uses a walking stick with great effect as I found out. However they will soon leave the ship now. It is not very comforting to have to cart chairs round for somebody nearly a year younger than yourself and who joined up at the College later than you did. Three of our crowd in the "Agincourt" have gone to destroyers for a months instruction. We all do a turn in destroyers but I did not think they would start so soon as they have done. I wrote to Enid about leave but she does not think that she will be able to get leave when I get it as her matron thinks there will be much work then.

The Australian letters have an exasperating way of arriving. I got yours dated March 31st three days ago. The next day I got one from Copper dated February 17th and none in between have arrived yet.

Mr Miller our divisional Lieutenant is on leave at present and Jack Rayment and I are in charge of the division all on our own.

Hope you got your holiday to Port Stephens.

Your affectionate son
JohnMArmstrong

HMAS Australia
May 26th 1918

Dear Mother

Thanks very much for your long letter. I got a bunch of letters from Australia on Monday last but there are still some missing I think. I am afraid that they have gone down or been lost somehow. The old crowd say that it is quite a common thing for letters to go astray after they have reached England. Sometimes they turn up a couple of months later sometimes they don't.

How is the cat getting on now, you said in your letter that she was not well.

I imagine that Dad had a very pleasant trip with Mr Busby. I would not mind at all if I could get out of Sydney for a week end on the harbour again but until they have direct aeroplane passenger service with this side there does not seem much chance of my doing it.

The Germans have begun their second offensive and I hear we have lost some slight ground I wonder how it will end.

Enid expects to get her leave in a couple of week's time. I wish we could get off together but that is impossible I think. I hear that Jersey is in quarantine for some reason and no naval ratings are permitted to go there. This puts a stopper on my going over there if the restrictions are not withdrawn by July. I hope very much that they will be withdrawn. Apart from the fact of not seeing the St Ouens people I would not know what to do with myself. Fourteen days spent at Leicester would be very dull as Enid would only be able to get off for a couple of hours a day.

Mr Miller the Lieutenant of my division has just returned from leave. He has been over to Ireland. It seems that lots of N.C.O's used to go over to Ireland for leave because it is not rationed. However it is harder to get over now as they have to get Passports.

We had another route march last week otherwise nothing out of the usual routine happened. The Aerodrome near here had some sports and four Australian snots got a second in the officer's relay race. Jack Rayment was one of them. Our own ships sports are to be held about the middle of next month. We are getting into training for it but I don't know quite what I am going to do for one. There is also a cutter race coming off soon but there are only a couple of midshipmen in the crew.

All ships are practicing for boat races and on a fine afternoon the Firth is dotted with boats. Different ships challenge one another to private races and the boats are followed by a host of noisy small craft from their respective ships. If the race comes off in the dog watches as it usually does the crews of other ships line the side and cheer them on.

Will you wish Dad Many Happy Returns of the 28th May for me please. I am sorry it is so late.

Your loving son
JohnMArmstrong

HMAS Australia
June 9th 1918

Received August 5th, 1918
Dear Mother

I have just got a long letter from you it came all by itself but there ought to be some more following. We have just returned from a mine laying stunt which proved very uneventful. We thought on going out that we might see something for a change but it was just the same old North Sea all the time which with never a ship in sight other than our own gets a bit monotonous.

You ask if I would like parcels sent thanks very much but I really don't need them as we get as much as we want and more in the way of sugar and chocolates. We get chocolates from Cadbury's at pre war prices. Cadburys only make them for the Army and Navy now. In many ways Enid wants parcels much more than I do. She can't get any sugar while we have as much as we want for porridge, tea, etc. Some things would rather likeare butter and honey. You can get tinned butter sent. We get plenty of jam and as often or not it is strawberry.

Those socks you knitted for me are wearing very well, though it has been too hot to wear them for some time now. Did you win any of your raffles?

The Germans have just begun a third offensive. I hope we can hold it this time. They will be jolly near Paris if they do as they have done in the two previous ones. I got a letter from Aunt Amy last week. They are all very well and want to know when I can get over to see them. Our time for docking has been put off so I don't know when we will get our leave, not till the end of September I expect. On the whole I am glad it has been put off as at present there are restrictions on people going to Jersey owing to Jersey having been in quarantine. However I hope the restrictions will have been withdrawn by then.

Enid goes on leave just about now. She said something about going to Devonshire. It ought to be glorious there just now. It is a pity our leave could not be made to fit in. However I will be able to put in a couple of days at Leicester.

Three of us went for a bicycle ride this afternoon. We hired the bicycles at a shop in Queensferry and of all the old boneshakers I ever saw they were the worst. We rode off towards Edinburgh and then turned off to a little village called Cramond on the waters edge. On entering the village we came to a steep hill with a very sharp turning at the bottom. Royston who was leading found his breaks would not act and hopped off to avoid hitting the wall at the foot of the hill. He was going quite fast and came a nasty cropper taking the skin off one of his hands whilst his bicycle smashed a couple of spokes.

Some people very kindly bandaged it up for him and after tea he was quite able to ride back. We came back to Queensferry by a track along the side of the Firth through the grounds of Dalmey Castle. After leave if I have enough money left I think I will buy myself a bicycle. At present I am saving up for leave. Sorry there is not more news.

Your affectionate son
JohnMArmstrong.

Midshipman John Malet Armstrong (1900-1988)

HMAS "Australia"
June 23rd 1918

Received August 19th 1918

Dear Dad

Many thanks for your letters. So far the mails from your side have arrived fairly regularly but we have heard that one from England had been sunk. I can't tell you the dates.

That was a very good photo of Holah (?) you sent me. I have sent mother a group of the Australian members of the Gunroom and some photos taken on a route march. I am also going to send you some photos taken on the trip over in the Beltana when I can get them printed. The negatives belong to Jack as all mine spoilt.

We have had several changes in our work. Four of the junior division of our mob have been put on Engineering for two months and they are complaining all the time about being overworked etc and all they seem to do is come up and sit on their chests. I am with Mr Manx the torpedo Lieutenant for action and so far the work has been very interesting. I go back to X turret when the original torp snottie comes off engineering. At sea I take my watch as snottie of the Watch instead of being lookout so I will have to try my hand at cocoa making not that it is very hard as cocoa is nearly always provided in the Ward Room at any time of night when at sea. The Commander is still on leave but he will be back any day now. I wish I could get as long leave as he has. He has been away for nearly a month now. However I suppose he has been saving up his leave for years.

Free postage has come in for the navy now so every one is trying to sell stamps. If you bought up all the stamps offered for sale at the prices asked and sold them ashore you would make a small fortune.

Enid is on leave at present. It was a pity we could not both get off together but my leave is so uncertain that it was not worth while her risking missing hers. The latest buzz going round is that we dock in the early part of August. So far I have not heard if Jersey is out of Quarantine but it ought to be by now. We have gone into Quarantine for Scarlet Fever a Signalman had it and did not report ill till he was almost delirious and he died in hospital two days afterwards. Being in Quarantine only means that we cannot visit or be visited by people from other ships and it does not affect leave at all.

We go north for the Quarterly Big Shoot next week I expect. I have not heard the big guns go off yet. I will most probably have to be outside and just above X turret on the aft super structure I have got myself a pair of ear protectors. I will probably be spotting fall of shot (not our own but those of the ship which uses us as a target) I may say that it is fixed so that the shots will not come aboard us but as they pitch fairly close it is comparatively easy to spot.

We had a cricket match on Saturday against the Ward Room and got badly beaten by three hundred odd to just over one hundred. Our bowling was our weak point as Reilly our crack bowler got a full pitcher on the head while we were batting and he had to retire for some time. We he went on to bowl he was naturally rather rocky.

I believe old Billy Hughes is coming on board to visit us and bringing Joe Cook along with him. We have to go out and do some stunts just for him. Just my luck when I wanted to go up to Edinburgh this week. Sorry I can't give you more news about what we are doing but it is "stricklich verboten" or whatever the correct thing is.

Your affectionate son
JohnMArmstrong

HMAS "Australia"
June 30th 1918

Received 13th September 1918
Dear Mother

Many thanks for you letter. I got an Australian mail this morning. It has been a coincidence that the last four Australian mails have arrived on Sunday morning in the middle of a large coaling.

We are up north now having arrived here at two in the morning after being at sea for several days so the ensuing coaling was a big one.

I must wish you Many Happy returns of the 5th of September. This will probably reach you a week or so before your birthday but I don't want to be late.

I have not been ashore here yet but what one can see of it is bad enough. There in not a tree to be seen anywhere and I believe the only tree in the islands is in the large village which is called Kirkwall a place of about two hundred houses and with Glasgow the only scotch town to own a real old cathedral if it is a very small one. The people who live here have to work like niggers to get enough to live on as the land is so poor. Just at present the weather is very fine for this part of the world we are told. It certainly is very pleasant. Crisp, but not too cold, and even hot in the sun.

The Torpedo work is very interesting and I think I am rather lucky to get the job for the time being. If you have actually done the thing it is a lot easier to remember for the exams. We want all the time we can get for torpedo work as it is the subject in which people generally fail.

There is a lot of work to get through on the practical side for the subs exam as we only have eighteen months to get hold of three years work.

Our big shoot comes off sometime this week I think. I will be in the conning tower and have practically nothing to do except to log data about the position of the "enemy" with regard to the chance of a hit with the "mouldies" The "enemy" will be the second subdivision of our squadron.

You asked in your last letter if there was anything I would like sent. Well I would like to see a Sydney paper now and again, could you let me have the Sun when you are sending papers to Enid please. We get the Bulletin so there is no use in sending that but I would like to get some general Sydney news now and again. Good night for the present as I am rather tired and we have to get under way early tomorrow.

Your affectionate son
JohnMArmstrong

HMAS "Australia"
July 8th 1918

Received 12th September 1918
Dear Dad

Many thanks for your last letter you seem to have had a very busy week. We have also been rather busy but I am sorry that I cannot give you an account of our doings. It seems that I have let you have a lot of information about our doings which would have been deleted by a censor. You understand that our letters are not censored, one of the Subs initials them and we are to see that nothing which might be censored is put in them. So far I have been writing a lot of things which I find are taboo. It's a good thing I found it out before someone else did. I am afraid that in consequence my news will deteriorate.

I met three of our crowd from the Agincourt on Wednesday, Hollingworth, Tate & Dudley. They are quite chirpy about things now and seem to have found their place in their Gunroom.

There is a "cage" going in the Gunroom at present about Australian politics. Poor old Billy is being called a fool by one lot and others stick up for him, there will be a scrap in a minute and I think I will knock off till the atmosphere is quieter.

A notice has been sent round to all Australians in the Grand Fleet to the effect that anyone who wishes to may volunteer for the Australian Air Service. Officers and men are both wanted. Several of our crowd have sent their names in but I did not think it was worthwhile. First of all after six months training you may find that you have not got the "nerve" and then so much time is wasted, secondly it is a young mans job and after about thirty you are not much good for flying. The only thing you can do is retire or become one of the Administrators. As more than half the Air Force are officers in the same circumstances there will be an enormous number of candidates for the Administrative. Under the circs I did not think it good enough. Then if you did get in there is always the chance of being put in an observation balloon department which would not suit my book at all. I don't think that any of my special friends have put their names down for it.

You asked how I was getting on for money. Up to date I am doing quite comfortably. When I arrived in England I drew on your credit for £ 25 as you know and put it to my own account. I used £ 7 for a uniform and another £ 10 while I was on leave in London. We are paid £ 8 a month and every three months we get the balance which makes it up to £ 12 minus any slops for that month. Out of the ordinary £ 8 my mess bill is from £ 4-10 to £ 5 and I used £ 2 a month on personal expenses. Which means that I save £1 on an ordinary month and £4 every quarter. To date I have £ 6 saved. For the next leave I will have about £ 20 at the least and I will not be long in town. It will be more than enough.

As regards uniform I will not want much new gear till next year when our uniform allowances of a bob a day begins.

I got a letter last week from Miss Austin a sister of Mr Bray who knows Allan Bellamy. They want me to go out and see them at their place at Hendon when I am next on leave. They have also intimated to Australia House that they will be very glad to entertain any Australian snotties who care to look them up.

No one knows the exact date of our refit yet and most probably wont till the day arrives.

And I don't know when I can get those photos done that I promised you however I will let you have them when I can.

Your affectionate son
JohnMArmstrong

Midshipman John Malet Armstrong (1900-1988)

HMAS "Australia"
July 21st 1918

Received ? October, 1918
Dear Mother

Many thanks for your letter. I am sorry to hear about Major Brownell and hope he is better again by now. The socks you made for me before I left are wearing very well and will last, with the others I got, all through next winter so don't bother to send me a whole new set.

Enid seems to have had a good leave. She has been as you most probably know all through Devon and generally had a good time of it. It was a pity our leaves could not be made to fit in. However mine is so jolly uncertain that it was not worth while Enid's putting hers off. The latest date for leave is September 10th but only extreme optimists put any faith in it.

Jack Rayment and Vail have both gone to Destroyers for a month's course. The destroyer's course is generally looked upon as a good thing. Jack joined his destroyer just as she went on "boiler clean" so that he got three days leave except for the fact that he had to sleep on board. Frank McMahon has just finished his destroyer's course and although he only had four days in harbour during the whole time he enjoyed every minute of it. He got stuck on the mud once, and spent some time on the Murman Coast up in Russia.

Miss Austin a sister of Mrs Bray who knows Allan and Ken wrote to me last week asking me to look them up next time I go to London. I have been having my teeth seen to in Edinburgh. I had to get a back tooth taken out as it was too decayed and too much "stopped" to stop again.

We played cricket against the "Lion" on Thursday up in Edinburgh on the "Grange" cricket ground. It was officers v officers. I was playing although I only just got in. We won by over a hundred runs.

Pely our sub of the Gunroom mess made over a hundred not out himself. My bowling has gone off sadly and they don't even put me on as a change bowler now. I think it is the want of practice.

The Americans gave a concert-show on Saturday evening. It was a revue, concert, funny party all roled into one. They had some parts of Chu Chin Chow and it was very well done. In fact the whole show was extremely creditable to a ships company. Sorry I can not give you any news of our doings mais c'est la guerre.

Your affectionate son
JohnMArmstrong

HMAS "Australia"
July 28th 1918

Received 9th October 1918
Dear Dad

What do you think of the war news now? It looks a little better than it did. The Americans seem to be throwing their weight about a bit.

We had a big coal on Thursday of nearly a thousand tons. I had been on watch most of the night before so I was jolly tired by the time we had finished.

It is Enid's birthday today. I wonder how she has been spending it. In her last letter to me she had been punting on the river, which river I can't say, and seemed to enjoy it. I am sorry to say there is very little news I can give you.

The King inspected the Grand Fleet Monday last and held an investiture on board the Flagship. The Zeebrugge decorations were given. Mr Boddie, do you remember him? He and Mr Stapleton took Enid & Margie Foster for a walking trip from the spit to Manly. When he was in charge of the engine room of the "Thetis" and when the engine room had been so badly damaged that the men were ordered to leave the place.

Mr Boddie volunteered to return and with some others got the engines moving again and she was able to carry on till she ran aground. He got the D.S.O. and was recommended for early promotion. A W.O seaman and a stoker got medals from the Australia. The W.O.'s being a D.S.C and the others D.C.M.'s. The W.O. was in the destroyer that kept the Vindictive alongside the mole and was responsible for the Engine room.

Your affectionate son
JohnMArmstrong

HMAS "Australia"
August 4th 1918

Received 9th October 1918
Dear Mother

What do you think of the war news now. Not so bad is it? A jolly good beginning for the 5th year of war. Of course everyone here is very pleased over it all, and it ought to buck your people up somewhat.

From your letters they seem to have painted things very black out there but people in England as far as I can see did not seem to mind very much, and took things quite calmly.

The threatened munitions strike looked rather bad but when the Government said that all who did not go back to work would be conscripted for the Army the whole thing fell through. In any case the men's leaders were against it. I got a letter from Dad on Saturday, which makes only two for the last three mails so I am afraid some have gone astray although Enid seems to have got fairly big mails. I could not quite understand Dad's letter as he referred to a strafing he had given me in a previous letter which has not arrived yet. He also mentioned some chocolates which have also not arrived. Well if the strafing and the chocolates arrive together they will mitigate each other although I have racked my brains to find out what sins I have committed. By the way Dad seems to think that the sweets might be considered rather juvenile. May I inform him that it is not so. In fact they will be very acceptable.

We had another big coal yesterday. Thank goodness it is the last for some time for me as I am going on a six weeks engineering course. I knock off duty and take on below. So far it has been very interesting. Mr Mabey is in charge of us but I have more to do with Mr Meyers the senior Watch keeping Engineer. He is a very decent sort and takes a great interest in us snotties.

Jack Rayment and Vail are returning from their destroyers after only doing two weeks although I don't know why as a month is the usual time.

Royston another of our crowd is going to a destroyer on Monday.

The squadron regatta is to be held sometime towards the end of this month and the snots have a whaler crew in for the Junior officers race. I am rowing, we have not had much training so far but then neither have the other ships. I am also going in for the Battle Cruiser junior officers boxing, but I don't know which weight I will be in.

Australia House was opened yesterday and two Australian snots went down for it although what they were wanted for is more than I can say. The lucky two got almost a weeks leave out of it as they had to go down some days ago the ship being "not available". We have had a busy couple of weeks lately and everyone is looking forward to leave but it is still as remote as ever. Would you mind getting a college magazine and sending it on to me please? It ought to be coming out at the end of August. I am in hopes of getting some more letters tomorrow so Dad's may be in that.

Your affectionate son
JohnMArmstrong

HMAS "Australia"
August 18th 1918

Dear Dad

We got a very big Australian mail this week and very welcome it was too. I have four of your letters to answer but some of Mother's have miscarried as I only got one and that was really a post script.

We don't want anything in the way of delicacies but woollens I should be very pleased to get, Mr Setting is quite right about the parcels, we get everything we want in the way of eatables, smokes etc on board at pre-war prices. Mr Setting was also right about Cunningham I am sorry to say, but of course I cannot give you any details.

I am very sorry about not seeing Uncle Edward, it was my fault that we did not see him the first week end in London. It was so unexpected that Enid only had time to get a wire to Uncle Tancred and did not even get an answer to that. Then while we were in town I rushed her round and generally managed things myself, so that I am really to blame and not Enid.

The second week end, Enid telegraphed to Uncle Edward beforehand but got no answer then when we went to Australia House he was away for the Easter Leave. I assure you though Dad that there was no Camouflage about it, Enid did her best to get hold of him the second week end and any negligence was mine.

I have not yet got that parcel of sweets you sent me but it is the usual thing to get parcels anytime up to six or eight weeks after they are expected. Perhaps it is rather a good thing that they have not come yet as the Boxing tournaments come off, one tomorrow and another next week.

Talking about the launch of the "Adelaide", Sir J Cook in a speech here said that "Of course he could not give details but the new Australian ship would be a powerful and useful help to the British Navy". It sounds very funny to us here were the "Sydney" and co were classed as old cruisers, (I hope the censor won't get on to me for the above)

I am glad old "Mangerton" is looking well it would grieve me very much to hear of anything happening to it. I am sorry to say I cannot keep a very precise log, as we are not permitted to in war time but I do my best with a small pocket book.

I hope Holak is better again he must be getting rather old now.

Jack Rayment and Vail are both back from their destroyers and quite disappointed to get back at first, but they have settled down again now. They had a vey good time. When in harbour got as much leave as they wanted and when at sea although they had to work hard, they enjoyed every minute of the work. Must be very interesting and I am quite looking forward to my Destroyers course. Although I hope it is not in the middle of winter.

The Grand Fleet Junior officers boxing comes off tomorrow and Tuesday. It is to be held on board the "Canada". I am in for it although my main objective in the boxing line is in the Battle Cruisers J.O.' tournament which is to be held in about a week to two weeks time. Whilst training I was boxing with one of the boys and got my nose boxed about a bit. However it is all right again and I hope will not get very badly damaged tomorrow.

The last year's lot made such a name for themselves at boxing that the R.A.N. counts a good bit so they say. It was Setting that did most of it. He won the heavies and most of his wins were knockouts. Anyhow whatever happens tomorrow I will be able to have a long talk with the Aussies in the "Canada" and most probably a number of the "Agincourt" will be over there too.

The seniors are working very hard for their Subs exam now. It is to be held at the end of the month. I hope they do well. It is a pity Mr Darley is not here to coach them up. He was never tired of helping the Australian Snots so they tell me.

The Right Hon. Sir J. Cook paid us a visit of state yesterday. We marched past him and afterwards he made a short speech. Then he visited the Ward Room, Gunroom, and Warrant officers mess and shook hands with everybody.

Mr Hughes seems to be talking a lot over here. Some of the papers simply hate him. While the Northcliff Press can't say too much for him. One paper had letters to the editor from people who wanted to get up subscriptions to enable him to a) To pay the legal expenses of his libel suit, b) To stay over here and go into the English parliament. It made me wild to see them. He gets up and talks a lot about what the Empire must do and what it must not do just as if he were the Prime Minister of England. The Northcliff press used him last time he was over here to beat the Asquith government with but what they want him now I can't see.

Leave is still ahead but not looming much nearer. We are training for the J.O. Whalers race in 2nd BCS regatta. And the 2nd BCS sports are to be held tomorrow. Of course I cannot go in for the sports as I am boxing but Jack and some of the others are going to try their luck.

I like the Engineering very much but my head is still sore from being bumped. There are certainly some disadvantages about being tall.

Your affectionate son
JohnMArmstrong

HMAS *"Australia"*
August 26th 1918

Received 29th October 1918

Dear Mother

Many thanks for your letters. I am afraid one of them has been lost as I have not yet got the one that you posted on June 2nd only your post script of June 3rd. Also the parcel which Dad sent me has not come yet, but then no one else has got any for some time. I think they are very careful with parcels now as people have been in the habit of sending bombs and such like contraptions.

We have had quite an eventful week. On Monday the first round of the J.O.B. contest were held. I won my first bout but was beaten in the afternoon by a fellow named Morson. He was about my weight but a much better boxer and I was quite glad when the three rounds were over.

The boxing was held in the "Canada" where some of our fellows are and they nearly all went in for it. I could not get over for the semi finals and finals on Tuesday which was a pity as I hear they were very good. MacKenzie, a snot of the year senior to us won the Heavyweights and a fellow named Arbuthnot got the Middles. I have not heard how our fellows got on in the other weights but I should think they would give a good account of themselves.

The squadron sports were held on Monday but of course I could not do anything in them as I was boxing. Jack Rayment and Vail came second and third in the Junior officers race which meant three points to us. The Australia won the cup for the greatest number of points scored rather easily. We got 44 points. The Indom 28, the Infex 26 and N.Z. 4. The N.Z. who is not our chummy ship was wild over it. This good win was largely contributed to by two P.O.'s of the torpedo division who between them won the hundred yards, the 220, the 440 and came first and second in the mile.

On Friday the squadron regatta was held but the Australia did not distinguish herself. We won only two races out of eighteen. Our snotties whaler only got fourth place in the Junior officers race which annoyed us mightily as we had been rather cock-sure over it. The Indom and Infex got 38 points the N.Z. 35 and ourselves 33 so we were not hopelessly outclassed.

On Saturday afternoon I went over to Glasgow with Morgan. He has a brother wounded and in hospital there so he goes over as often as he can. The train takes an hour and ten minutes to get there and you have about an hour and a half in the town. I saw Maggie, she was very well and seemed very happy. She and her husband live in a small flat *in a place called Patrick West. They have been looking for another and larger place for some time but Maggie tells me that you have to bribe the estate agents to get any sort of place at all.*

They were very pleased to see me and send their best wishes to you and Dad.

When I got back to the ship I found a note from one of the judges of the boxing to say I had won a good losers prize at the boxing. It is a silver pencil with "Good boxer 1918" engraved on it.

Our leave is rumoured to be some time in October now. The Lion has done us in for our place. The trouble is that our machinery and the ship herself is in such good repair that there is no hurry for our docking and any ship needing repairs beats us for it. You know it is rather good considering that we have been in commission for over five years and the makers said that a lot of gear would probably have to be renewed by four years time from her first commissioning.

The Admiral, Captain and Commander are all leaving at the end of the month. We are wondering who the new officers will be.

The senior snots are in the middle of their subs exam now. So far everyone on Australia had been successful. I suppose they will be leaving in a months time, and we will be the senior snots in the Gunroom. They may send some juniors here but we are rather hoping that they don't till the next year comes over from Australia.

I am still on engineering and find it very interesting also we generally manage to escape coaling, however I think that I would rather be a Deck officer.

Pelly the Sub of the Mess is due for his second stripe next month. He was in Philip's term at Dartmouth and so he knew him quite well.

Your loving son
JohnMArmstrong

HMAS "Australia"
September 15th 1918

Received 16th December 1918
Dear Mother

Admiral Levison left the ship at the beginning of last week. He is to get command of a much better squadron than ourselves. He of course took his staff with him so we have a complete change of staff. Our new Admiral is R. Admiral Halsey and Captain James is his flag Captain.

We had a couple of games of football this week. The first was a ships team against the "Dublin". They wanted four snots and as the seniors are still finishing their exams they chose four of us. It was a good game

163

the "Dublin" winning 12-3. The ground was a caution, half an inch of mud all over it and dried heather stalks mixed up with the mud which cut you about. However it was pleasant to play again. Another time we were to have played the N.Z. officers team but they had a prior match, Ward Room v Gun Room so we went ashore and had a pickup with some of the matloes.

On Thursday I went for a walk with Casey and Jack Rayment and walked over to the other side of one of the islands. It is a very bare place, no trees and not much grass.. Except where the ground is cultivated it is all covered with heather. The farm houses are built of stone and thatched with what appears to be peat. We had tea in one of them and a jolly good tea too. Fresh butter, eggs and hot scones all for a bob, quite different from the mainland.

I got a photo of Enid yesterday in her nurses uniform, quite a good one but somehow different from the others that I have seen of her lately.

Our leave is just as far off as ever but perhaps it is a good thing as Enid may be able to get leave at the same time and we could both get over to Jersey. We are expecting to have a lot of work soon so the leave will be farther off than ever.

I am sorry there is not more news for you but things are pretty humdrum at present except for purely service matters, sometimes they are quite exciting.

The war news is better nowadays, looks as if the tide has turned at last.

Your loving son
JohnMArmstrong

HMAS "Australia"
September 22nd 1918

Received 19th December 1918
Dear Dad

What do you think of the war news now, everyone is very jubliant over it here.

I have taken over a new job now. We finished our Engineering course on Friday. It has been very interesting and I liked the work but I do not think I should like to take it up. They are not going to make anyone take up engineering who has been through the College although you can if you want to.

The method of supplying engineers is through University now. Mr Mabey who is an engineer lieutenant has been generally in charge of us during the course. He is a Sydney University man and knew Edwin *and Lloyd Hutchinson. He was in the same year as Edwin at the Varsity. We all like him very much.*

My new job is "Tanky" ie Commander N's doggie. My duties are to wind, compare and rate chronometers every morning and at sea I should be on the bridge whenever the Commander N is but Commander Crichton who is our new navigator only requires me on entering or leaving harbour, when in sight of land and during the forenoon at sea. My duties at sea are to take times and courses etc and I also keep an old chart and plot our position on it and take sights when I get a chance. While at sea I have quite a lot to do but it is Independent work and I much prefer it to watch keeping. Also if the Commander N is not in a bad temper he usually lets me stand off coaling. A great boon here, where it is nearly always raining and very often windy.

On Thursday afternoon I went ashore with Anderson and played a game of golf on the course built by the fleet. I was very dud at first but managed to hit the ball on the first attempt when we got on a little way. You are not very noticeable if you cannot play as everybody goes in for it. Anderson is quite good at it and beat me by twelve holes on the eighteen hole course.

This afternoon there was a panic in one of the Cutters and I could not go as I had a watch however I was very glad I did not before the afternoon was over as it came on to rain hard and got very cold.

Mr Pope who was a lieutenant at Geelong and is now in the Sydney has been married to an Australian over here. Mr Darley has left Whale Island some time now and is I believe in one of the light cruisers.

Your affectionate son
JohnMArmstrong

HMAS "Australia"
September 29th 1918

Received 23rd December 1918
Dear Mother

This last week we have had a very busy time at sea nearly all the time in fact there has not been a day during which we have not done at least twelve hours steaming.

I have had a lot of work and like my new job very much. I am supposed to be on the bridge all the time Commander N. is there but he usually tells me to have the night in my hammock. He personally sleeps in the lower chart house and is called for any thing unusual or for an alteration of course so he has a pretty rough time of it at sea. To make up for it he does practically nothing in harbour.

When we have been out for some time Commander N. gives me permission to stand off coaling much to the envy of the other snots. On the whole it is a much more independent job than snot of the watch to say nothing of being more interesting. You know exactly what is going on.

The Australians in the "Canada", "Royal Sovereign" and "Glorious" have all passed their exams for Sub Lieutenant except two who however having passed seamanship will be Acting subs until they can sit for the subject in which they failed. The senior snots in the "Australia" are very anxious to hear how they have done. I hope they do well.

I believe that there will be something doing in the near future as the Germans seem to be clearing out of the Belgian harbours and they may come out in force to escort their destroyers back. One never knows but you would not think that the old hun will leave them without a covering force.

We are expecting a large mail from Australia shortly as nobody has had any Australian letters for nearly a month. By the way do you remember my telling you that I had not got a letter you wrote to me about Uncle Edward. It is very funny as I got the one which Dad had posted at the same time and the one you sent me a day later.

Your affectionate son
JohnMArmstrong

HMAS "Australia"
October 6th 1918

Received 23rd December 1918
Dear Dad

We have had another busy week, at sea practically the whole time. The hun did not come out in force as was expected to escort his little ships from the Belgian coast, I believe they slipped out one at a time and so got through. We would have got him on the hop if he had.

The war news is getting better and better every day. Now it looks as if the war will not last much longer at any rate more than another year. That is the general opinion over here, in fact people are getting quite optimistic. I heard a bet given last week that the war would be over before Christmas but I hardly think it will be as good as that. There was great jubilation in the ship on Monday last. At 9.p.m the Chief boatswains Mate was heard bawling at the top of his voice. "Hear This, Bulgaria has surrendered unconditionally" He was piping it round the Mess deck. Everybody cheered like mad.

The Commander N. is leaving us soon. He is going to the Q.E. as navigator and will be Master of the Fleet. Of course it is the best place he can get. I believe admiral Beatty wrote personally for him. I went ashore this afternoon for a walk and had tea at one of the farmhouses. You can get a better tea up here than any where down south. It is the only place in England or Scotland where fresh butter is procurable in any quantity without coupons and permits.

Our leave is still quite remote. There is one straw which some grasp at. Captain James is going to be married in the last week of October so the wise people say that we must be going on leave about that time.

Your affectionate son
JohnMArmstrong

P.S. If mother is sending anymore socks or something like that would you mind slipping in a tin or two of Vice Regal Mild or Medium I can't get any over here and it is the one I like best.

St Ouens Manor
November 3rd 1918

Received in Australia 26th December, 1918
Dear People

I am sorry I did not write last Sunday but as you will see we have been very busy. To begin, during the week before last we carried on much the same as usual, nothing of note happened as usual. On the Thursday we played the NZ's gun room rugby and won fifteen-nil. The match was a very good one. Their forwards were mostly public school snots and it took us all our time to hold them.

We had tea at the golf house afterwards and yarned to the NZ's snots. None of their lot passed their sub exams, they all failed on one of the gunnery papers (Jock became Gunnery officer of HMAS Australia, the county class cruiser in WW2)

We got the final news about the subs exam too. Two out of seven failed to pass this gunnery exam but as they had passed seamanship they are all acting subs. Reilly one of the two who failed had very bad luck. He got four "firsts" out of six subjects and then failed in the most important Gunnery paper. As it was his total percentage for gunnery was 84. The Captain and Admiral are doing their best to get him through.

On the Friday we were told unofficially that our leave and in fact all Grand F leave had been indefinitely postponed and on the same evening I got a letter from Enid to say that she was ill with the "Flu" but she was getting better again. On Sunday last at midday it was piped around the ship that we were going into dock on Monday morning. You can guess our excitement. We began raising steam at once and Admiral

167

Halsey hastely got all his gear and staff over to the NZ and we steamed out of Scapa with band playing and ship company lining the side, just as it was getting dark. We arrived at Rosyth by eight next morning and by ten we were in the dock. I came south by the leave train which got into London at three am on Tuesday morning. Together were five of us and we could not get a room anywhere so we camped in the smoking room of Euston station. I went off by the 8.30 train for Leicester and went up to see Enid in the afternoon. She was still in bed and will be for a week or so, but she was looking much better than expected. She was rather thin but had most of her colour back. Miss Brennan was also down with flu. It appears that Enid had been ill with flu for three or four days before she went to bed with it. They had been short handed in her ward, reported to the matron as being ill. They sent her to bed at once and there she is.

I put up at the Grand Hotel in Leicester and sat with Enid as much as I could. I spent Wednesday there and as Enid was well on the mend decided to go over to Jersey as soon as possible.

I left Leicester on Thursday morning and arrived in London at midday only to find on enquiring at Waterloo that the boat for Jersey did not leave till Friday night. I took my gear to the Australian Club and went off to see Uncle Edward. He was suffering from very slight flu but not enough to keep him indoors. We had lunch at the Cheshire Cheese and then I paid a visit to the bank to draw the rest of my £ 25. In the afternoon Uncle Edward took me down to the Author'Club and spent quite an enjoyable time. We listened to some arguments about the war which were very interesting. Turkey surrendered unconditionally, and Austria is in a state of revolution. Some of the papers give what they think are Foch's terms for an Armistice with Germany and they are hard too. The Germans to lay down their arms and march back to Germany. We are to occupy German territory for thirty miles. For the German Fleet to hand itself over to the British Fleet, all prisoners of war to be returned at once. If Germany accepts them she will be having her nose rubbed in the dirt as no nation has ever been humiliated in history.

The evening I spent at the Australian and met a lot of officers I know. There were two of the new subs from the "Glorious", they had just had their appointments to destroyers. Then I met the older of the Payne boys. He was on leave from France. I also saw several officers who came over in the "Beltana". Friday morning I chased round town with Tompson one of the subs and we had a cocktail at the "Picadilly". The boat train left Waterloo at 2.30 and got down to Southampton at four. After a lot of parlarver about Passports which I escaped we were *allowed on board. I being an Officer was permitted to land again and had dinner in Southampton. We left at 1.00pm and I turned in at once.*

We had a very rough passage and I am sorry to say I was sick. The boat got into St Helier at 10am instead of seven. Uncle Rex was there to meet me and sent me up to the Manor at once. He himself had work in town. I got up to the manor in time for lunch. Everyone is well except Guy who is recovering from a weak heart and much to his disgust is not allowed to rush about.

Aunt Amy looks very well and so do Elley and Uncle Rex. The manor is looking bare as they have cut down all the ivy and the Virginia Creeper has not spread very much as yet.

All the servants are away with Flu so we do everything for ourselves and it is rather fun. Everyone sends you their love and wish to be remembered to you. I am sending Mother that Christmas card I spoke of. The picture is of Australia firing.

Your loving son

HMAS Australia
November 13th 1918

Dear Mother

We are back again on board after a most enjoyable leave and fourteen days of most excitable events. In my last letter I had just arrived in Jersey. Guy and Elley still have to be careful of their hearts but otherwise everyone was very well. All Aunt Amy's servants are away with Flu so we did all our own housework. Or rather Elley did most of it. The ivy has been cut down from the manor as it was blocking up the drains and it makes the place rather bare otherwise it has not changed as far as I can remember

On Sunday Uncle Rex, Elley and I went down and visited cousin Marie (my great grand aunt?) at "Bon Air" but of course I did not remember her. On the Monday we went over to see some people called Rod. They live about the middle of the island. Elley and I walked and Aunt Amy and Guy drove in the pony cart. Uncle Rex called in on his bicycle. Mr Rod is an Australian and knows Uncle Tancred, at one time he was champion amateur boxer in Sydney. His sister taught Enid swimming. He has married a second time to a very pretty American girl. We talked a good deal about Australia and looked at Mr Rod's photos, he seems to have been almost everywhere at one time or another.

He has a son in the "Lord Nelson" a pre-dreadnaught which is stationed in the Mediterranean and the latest news was that they are likely to go up the Dardanelles soon.

On Wednesday we all had lunch with Sir R Vernon at St Peters House. Sir R is the head man of the Jersey court. St Peters House was very interesting being a sort of ancestral mansion.

On Wednesday (? does he mean Thursday) we were going for a picnic to the north of the Island but the people at the hotel were all down with the "Flu" so we went to St Brelades Bay instead. It was too cold to picnic out so we had lunch at the hotel and then Ellie, Guy and I went for a walk round the rocks. There is a little church yard there with some graves of the German prisoners of war whom there are a fair number in Jersey. They had chosen the most prominent spot in the whole churchyard right up against the road where they would be most noticeable.

Among the rocks was a huge cave which is said to be a prehistoric dwelling. They have been cutting away the rock looking for remains and the whole thing has been spoilt. There were some more ancient remains at St Ouens Bay, an old burying place after the manner of Stonehenge. We saw some of the shells of shellfish which had been put for some thousands of years ago for the late lamented to eat when they came too.

On Thursday (has he has lost a day somewhere?) we went down to St Helier and had lunch with Cousin Anne. She showed me Jack's Croix de Guerre. The latest news of Fred was that he would most probably have to stay out in Mesopotamia for about six months longer and he was not at all pleased about it as you can imagine.

On Friday it rained but cleared up for the afternoon and Elley, Guy and I went for a long walk along the top of St Ouen's Bay.

In the evenings we sat in Aunt Amy's room off the hall and talked. Elley was very keen to get news about the Navy and in fact so were Aunt Amy and Uncle Rex. They even talked occasionally about Philip and the Queen Mary. All except Aunt Amy dislike the Americans intensely. Elley was very bitter on the subject, she considers that they only entered the war to make what they could out of it and having come in at the end took all the credit to themselves. I rather stuck up for them and we had a long argument on the subject. I left on Saturday morning by the "Alberta" which had brought me over after having had a most enjoyable time. The sea was as calm as could be, very different from the former crossing. We called in at Guernsey and who should come aboard but Frank Benn. He had been on a weeks leave and was just returning. We had a long talk, he has been in France most of this year and described some of the fighting to me.

He knew the Captain of the "Alberta" and we went up to his cabin after dinner. The Captain said that he had not received any messages about submarines for over a week. They let us into Southampton at night to which they have not been doing since the U boat Campaign began. We slept on board and I caught a train on Sunday morning up to London.

Frank went off to Salisbury Plains. The train was very slow and did not arrive in London till midday. However the news in the papers was enough to keep anyone interested. Great headlines about the Kaiser's abdication and the meeting between Foch and the German delegates. I had lunch at the Australia Club and caught the afternoon train for Leicester where I found Enid out of bed but not very strong.

On the Monday morning I slept till nine o clock, and ordered a taxi for ten thirty so I wanted to take Enid for a joy ride if possible. The taxi man agreed to take us and said that I could always have business of sort on hand if any questions were asked. Just as it was leaving for the Hospital the news boys came running out of a newspaper office close to the Hotel with the news that the Armistice had been signed. Having picked Enid up we returned through the town and drove out to a small village about six miles out. Even then people were hanging out flags and when we got back Leicester was packed with people and flags were flying everywhere. We had dinner at my hotel and toasted the Armistice in champagne.

I had to leave by the six o clock train and arrived in London at nine and transferred myself and gear to Euston as our special train left at ten.

I had started out from Jersey with the idea of spending Sunday at Leicester and meeting Uncle Tancred on Monday but as things turned out it was just as well I did not. Euston was crammed with Australian soldiers and sailors. The "diggers" had come to see their pals off ie those of their pals who were able to leave. Two hundred found the armistice rejoicings too much for them and returned on board in detachments anything from twenty four to forty eight hours adrift. We arrived at Rosyth on midday on Tuesday. The ship was in the most appalling mess you ever saw. Mud inches thick on the decks and remains of scaffolding littered round which tripped one up and sent you head first into the mud. There have been numerous alterations, mostly as regards the magazines which have been made entirely flash proof.

We left the dock in the afternoon and moved in our usual position. The remainder of our squadron were down here so as soon as the ship was ammunitioned, coaled and comparatively clean Admiral Halsey transferred his flag to the NZ. I was running a picket boat and so escaped the coaling which was a rotten one although only a comparatively small amount to get in being short handed made it very long.

The men kept coming off in small parties by each train which came north and the picket boats met each one. To make things worse we have had perpetual fog for over a week. On the evening of the 11th ie the Armistice night the fleet "spliced the main brace" and sirens were going from six pm to 10pm. Of course I did not see it but I am told that the searchlights, rockets and verey lights were all going at the same time. The men who were only twenty four hours adrift were let off fairly easily as the Captain said that there was a certain amount of excuse for them. The snots who were in London for the Armistice day say that people almost went mad. The streets were packed and they had great difficulty in getting their gear and themselves from the Australian Club to Euston.

Jack Rayment who spent a week at Lady Northcotes place said they made them feel at home as soon as they stepped inside.

The "Koenigsberg" who is bringing the German delegates to Admiral Beatty is arriving on Friday.

Sunday 17th – We went to sea on Wednesday and I was not able to finish my letter.

We thought we were going to meet the "Koenigsberg" but we had no such luck and were only a covering force for the light cruisers and destroyers just to see that the Hun played no tricks. However when it was found that he was up to nothing we returned to harbour without even seeing him. In side the fog is still as thick as ever and although it lifted this afternoon I hear the bell going again now so I suppose it has come down again.

The "Koeningsberg" is rather was anchored below Burnt island which is further down the Firth than our anchorage. One of the RN subs who was on a destroyer which escorted her in says that when they met her they all circled round taking photos. He also says that the men were loafing round on deck and doing no work on board the "Koeningsberg". Admiral Beatty received the German admiral but refused to see the Workmens and Sailors delegates. He sent round a signal this afternoon which stated that the ships to be interned were ten of their newest battleships, all battle cruisers (6), and seven newest light cruisers and fifty destroyers and 160 submarines to be given up to us. The ships are to rendezvous with the Grand Fleet some time this week and will be taken to some harbour, examined and interned the harbour of internment is most probably Scapa Flow where they will be left with caretakers onboard. I have managed to get two unused films for my camera.

There are numerous buzes going round about our movements, by ours I mean the "Australia's". We hoisted our Australian Jack by special permission last week. The latest buzz and it seems fairly substantial is that fairly soon we go into John Brown's hands (he is the firm that built us) and do a long refit and then proceed to Australia picking up our cruisers which are here and our destroyers which are in the Mediterranean on the way and incidentally calling in at allied and neutral ports. Let's hope it is true.

Enid is not sure when she will be able to get out but she will let you know her rumours and plans. Three of our RAN subs who have left us. Two are doing a course at Whale Island and one is joining the "Huon"(?) a notice has been posted in the gunroom to the effect that any RN officers who do not wish to go to Australia are to give in their names as soon as possible.

The enclosed photo is taken from a Sunday paper. Might I mention that the "Koeningsberg" entered the Firth in a fog and left in a fog so I wonder where they got the sunlight.

Your affectionate son
JohnMArmstrong

HMAS Australia
November 24th 1918

Dear Dad

Many thanks for your letters. I got two from you and one from Mother on Monday last.

I have not got the parcels yet that you mentioned however any thing up to two months late is the usual thing.

We have had a most exciting time. The 21st was "Der Tag" to some tune. Up till Thursday it had been very foggy and we thought it would not clear up however it did much to everybody's satisfaction. We were lying below the Forth Bridge at the end of the Battle Cruiser line. At one in the morning we unmoored and weighed at three, We steamed out at the head of the line until outside May Island which marks the entrance to the Forth, where the whole fleet formed in two lines six miles apart, and the squadrons in reserve order so that when we turned about to return everybody would be in their right place. In this manner we advanced at 10 knots and about 8 am the head of our line which was the southern one signalled back that the German fleet was in sight.

We sighted the leaders at 9.40. The Cardiff a light cruiser led the German line and when she was abreast of our squadron we turned about and headed for the Forth in three parallel lines. The "Lion" led the Northern line and we led the Southern. The whole fleet was at action stations but all the guns were trained for and aft. When we arrived back at May Island which was about midday our lines turned outward and the Huns went on to their anchorage.

Our ships came in after them. The Huns anchored in the form of a square about twenty miles up the Forth and below the Fleet anchorage. The 1st Battle Squadron consisting of the Revenges the Iron Dukes and the Canada and our noble selves the second Battle Cruiser Squadron were the guard ships. We anchored outside the Huns. When we steamed up to our anchorage the Queen Elizabeth was some way ahead watching the ships coming in and as each ship passed they cheered the Commander in Chief. We went full speed to reach her before she moved off as Admiral Halsey wanted to cheer, however the C in C was not having any and went off at full speed himself.

As a result we overshot our berth and had to steam right round the German fleet so we had a very good view of them at close quarters and I got a couple of photos.

Each of the guard ships had to send an inspection party on board one of the Huns. We were told off for the "Hindenburg" one of the latest Battle Cruisers. I went to take notes for the Commander who is a German interpreter. They piped us on board and we were taken to the Admirals cabin. The admiral was not on board and a "Commander" was in command. This was the same all through the German fleet all the senior officers had been left behind. The German Commander was a typical Prussian and the atmosphere was rather strained. Our Gunnery Torpedo and Engineering parties were given guides and made a short inspection of their departments. Our Commander went round the upper deck and then gave the German Commander his orders.

The "Hindenburg" is a very fine ship and would be a good match for the "Tiger" although not up to the "Repulse" About half the crew were onboard the remainder being "on leave". A couple of petty officers wearing armulets with "arbeiter" und soldaten" on them seemed to have equal control with the officers. The crew were very orderly and saluted the officers when passing.

On Friday morning another party went onboard to make a more thorough inspection. I again went as the Commanders doggie and three other snots came as well having got various people to say they needed ADC. The Commander went all over the ship and I had to follow making notes on anything and everything.

Later on in the morning Admiral Halsey and fifteen or so brass hats came on board. I then went round on my own and tried to get a German ensign but there were none on the bridge so instead I pinched a signal with Workmens and Soldiers stamp on it. Before we went onboard we

174

were given strict orders to treat the Huns with the very barest civility which you may bet we did.

Some of the men tried to get into conversation with us but the officers were very aloof, and did not like it one little bit, In their wardroom they had a large portrait of the Kaiser in all his war paint. The tables were arranged in a half moon so that they would all face old Bill. The gunroom had Hindenburg in the place of honour. Their turrets are much larger than ours for the same size guns and the rangefinders were thirty two foot base while our largest is fifteen feet. Of course all the lenses had been taken out and certain of the important parts of the guns also.

Yesterday I got a number of snaps of the Huns but spoilt them in developing so I will try and get some more to send you.

Your affectionate son

Jock.

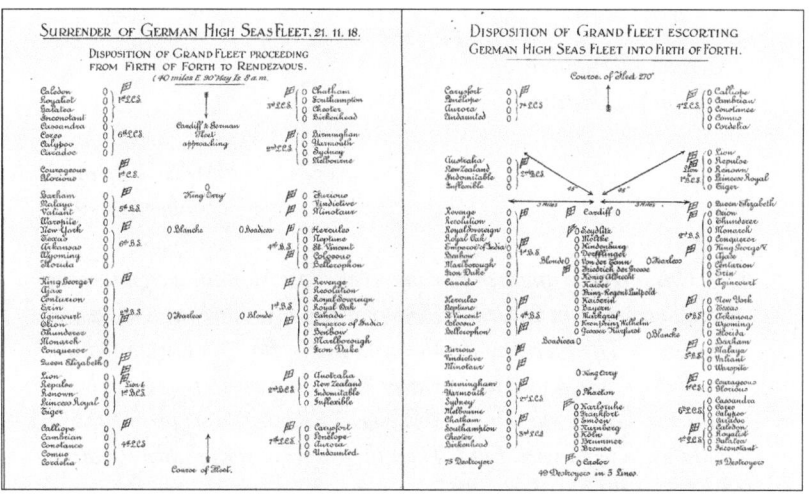

Plan of Surrender of the German Fleet (National Library of Australia)

HMAS *"Australia"*
December 1st 1918

Dearest Mother

We have had a comparatively quiet week after our recent excitements. On Sunday last I got a number of photos of the Germans as they lay at anchor but I am sorry to say I spoilt them all in the developer. It is a funny thing that ever since I left Australia I have not managed to get any good results with my tank. In future I am going to get all my photos developed ashore. I got two films done like this and they are quite

175

good. The ones of the Americans were taken fairly late in the Afternoon as a dull day which accounts for their being so thin. The ones of the manner were taken on leave.

All censorship restrictions were removed on letters and photos so I sent you a number of the ship taken by the official photographer who is a warrant officer and usually does fairly well. I will send you those he got of the Germans in place of the ones I spoilt, when he has them ready.

On last Sunday afternoon the German Battle Cruisers went to Scapa escorted by the 1st Battle cruiser squadron. On Monday half the German Battle ships followed them.

There are rumours of getting leave again. Christmas leave is to be given to the fleet, one watch at a time for ten days so very likely we will get leave again soon. Also there is talk of the Australia's going into dock for a long refit and then proceeding to Australia.!! I don't quite know how I shall get on if we do as it will mean lots of leave and buying new kit and my finances are rather low, however I am doing well and always have Dads letter of credit to fall back on.

Your affectionate son
JohnMArmstrong

HMAS "Australia"
December 8th 1918

Dear Dad

This has been another exciting week. Last Monday a signal came through from C. in C. Grand Fleet that ten days Christmas leave was to be given. The Fleet was divided into two sections, A section to have from 5th to 25th and B section after 25th. One watch is to go on leave at a time. Great was our joy and especially mine, as it meant that I would get a week with Enid. Then the Captain said that we snotties could have the twenty days!!!

I wired to Enid at once and we decided to spend a week in London as otherwise we would only have four days together in Jersey. Aunt Amy kindly wired to me to come over when, and for as long as I liked. I wrote off to the Commercial Bank and cashed the remainder of your letter of credit as I had a lot of gear to get and was broke from the last leave.

Then on Wednesday evening the following signal came through. "2nd B.C.S. will be probably required shortly for service in the Baltic and it is therefore regretted that Christmas leave must be postponed." Was it not a bombshell. We are standing by and it is even odds whether we go or not. Personally as we will not go on leave till January now in

*any case. I hope we go to the Baltic as it is very dull staying in harbour.
We coaled and oiled to full capacity on Thursday morning and we have
re-provisioned since. Also they have got a stock of winter gear onboard
which points to our going. However the Captain was heard to say that
he would give five to four that we would not go. I believe it depends on
the behaviour of the Bolshevics in the near future. One of our latest light
cruiser squadrons is in the Baltic and one of them the "Cassandra" struck
a mine and was lost yesterday. The remainder returned to Copenhagen.
That means if we do go it will not be till the minefields are known or
cleared away.*

*On Friday next the New Zealand is going to Bergen in Norway to
bring over the Queen of Norway.*

*A large Australian mail has just come in, two letters from you and
two from mother as well as numerous papers. You ask me if I have got
enough money, don't worry at all about that. None of us ever have a
superfluity of it but I personally have ample. I have cashed the second
£ 25 of your letter of credit but as we are not going on leave till next
year it will stand over and I shall not want any more. Leave especially
in London runs away with a lot but while onboard I can save about £
10 on the quarter.*

*We can get leave till ten o clock once a week if we want to but it is
not much good unless you have friends to go to.*

*Aunt Amy gave me the address of Mrs Leonard Malet who is living
in Edinburgh and will go and see her the first opportunity I get.*

*Yesterday a team from the New Zealand and ourselves played rugby
against one of the Edinburgh schools "Watsons" by name. It was a vey
good game and although we got badly beaten, twenty-three – nil, we
all enjoyed it very much. We were very much out of training and had
no organisation. As we can never get into real hard training the first
people up form down in the scrum so as not to keep the game held up,
this means that the scrum does not break up quickly and the opponents
halves have the ball to themselves and can always get it out to their
backs. If we had fixed places the breakaways could smother them and
we would have stopped most of their scoring. However our teams are
always scratch teams and it is not worth while.*

*I will be sending you or mother numerous photos and snapshots
from time to time. Would you please keep them as I would like to get
them into an album later on. An official photographer is on board
at present and has been taking films and photos of everybody and
everything. He took a photo of the officers and ships company of which
I will send you a copy as soon as they are ready,*

*All the R.A.N. subs except one have left the ship and gone to mine
sweepers or destroyers. Those on mine sweepers are getting £ 9 a week
and will continue to do so while engaged in sweeping. Pelly our sub of
the mess has been promoted to Lieutenant and one Pedder is now sub
of the mess. We all miss Pelly as he was one of the best subs we have ever
had or are likely to have. He was one of Philip's team at Dartmouth
and he was in the "Formidable" when she went down. (The Formidable
a Battleship was sunk by a U boat on 1st January, 1915 off the Devon
coast – nearly 550 men out of 780 were lost)*
    Your affectionate son
    JohnMArmstrong

                                                    St Ouens Manor
                                                    Jersey
                                                    December 13th 1918
Dear Mother
    *Very many thanks for the parcels you sent me. I got the Balaclavas
and honey which arrived in one lot and the cardigan jacket in another.
I also got the parcel from Mrs Jennings. The woollens are great, just the
thing I wanted*
    *I have got a couple of home letters which arrived by last mail, they
were sent just after the armistice and by all accounts you seem to have
had a very good time in Sydney. The Sydney mails also arrived with the
pictures of the celebrations. What a time you must have had.*
    *I arrived here on the 5th after a very good passage although the
boat was very much overcrowded. Everyone at the manor is very
well, Guy is still under Doctors orders for his heart but is rapidly
recovering.*
    *The Island has been very gay, Ellie has had seven dances already.
There was a small one held the day after I arrived and Uncle Rex had
got an invitation for me. It was great fun, Ellie introduced me to heaps
of girls and I had my program filled in no time. It was the first dance
of any size I have ever been too and I enjoyed it immensely, we were to
leave at one o clock but our taxi did not arrive till nearly two so we saw
the dance right out.*
    *Who do you think came over in the same boat as me? The Coxes,
they came up to the Manor on Thursday afternoon and I remembered
seeing them onboard, although I had not recognised them. They are
thinking of taking a house and living in the island, they like the climate
so much. Mrs Cox said they were going to see it at its worst before they
decided finally.*

On Wednesday afternoon I played in a hockey match, officers on leave v Victoria College. Harold Collet-White a friend of Guys who is spending the holidays at the Manor played for the College so we bicycled down together. The match was played on the sands of St Ouen's bay. Unfortunately some of the College team did not turn up. However we had a good game. Officers on leave winning by five goals to one.

There are two brothers Collet-White staying at the Manor. Their people are out in India and Guy has them to spend their holidays with him. The younger brother has some idea of entering the navy but he is rather delicate and I doubt if he would pass the doctors.

On Friday evening some of the members of Uncle Rex's club gave a large dance called the "antediluvian" as it was given by a lot of old "dugouts". The music was of twenty years ago and fox trotting etc did not come into the program. It was a top hole dance, I had my program full right off. Valerie Cox was there, she likes Jersey very much but I doubt if she wants to live here for good.

By the way I met Jack Marett whose sister you have seen something of. He had a weeks leave and is going back to a destroyer, he hopes to get to Cambridge fairly soon. I am having a ripping leave, Aunt Amy sends her love and asks when you intend to come over.

Your affectionate son
JohnMArmstrong

HMAS "Australia"
December 15th 1918, Rosyth

Received 26th February, 1919
Dear Mother

Very many thanks for your letters. I got a number of papers now from you last Sunday and jolly glad I was to get them, also a Lone Hand from Dad which had a very good article on the College.

I have not got the College magazine yet but as several others got it I was able to see all I wanted to, not that there was anything interesting in it this year.

Dad says in his last letter that by the time I get it the war may well be over well it is quite over a month now since it was over. None of the parcels you sent have arrived yet but large parcel mails are coming in every day. We are still standing by for the Baltic although I think that the show is off. It would have been better than swinging round our moorings as we are now. We got another leave shock yesterday. Vice Admiral Battle Cruiser force, Admiral Packenham made a signal to all Battle Cruisers that as many junior officers as possible were to be given Christmas leave. We all thought that it was quite the right spirit for "Pax" to show but the usual shock came soon afterwards in the shape of a signal "Re Junior officers Christmas leave, negative 2nd Battle Cruiser squadron".

Then I get a letter from Ellie mentioning that there will be a dance on the 27th and one again on the 5th and could I possibly wrangle leave.

There was a football match against "Watsons" college yesterday. They beat us badly when we played before so we determined to do better this time. However they won again but not by much this time and it was a very good game. The ground was very hard with the result that everyone was cut about, however they gave us a very good tea afterwards which made up for it.

Enid left Jersey yesterday so I suppose she is quite well again. It was a pity that we could not get on leave together but I suppose we will get belated Christmas leave and I ought to see something of her then. There is no more news as yet about our returning to Australia but I believe there is something in the wind. I am sorry there is not much news this week, things are very slow at present.

Your affectionate son
JohnMArmstrong

St Ouen's Manor
January 5th, 1919

Dear Dad

I have just got your letters about the armistice. You seem to have had a very gay time in Sydney. This is a two weeks letter as I am sorry to say, I missed the Sunday after Christmas. Last time I wrote we were thinking of going to the Baltic but on the 23rd it was definitely stated that our squadron should go on leave on the 1st January when the 1st B.C.S. came back from leave. There is an enormous amount of news for you and I don't quite know where to begin.

Just before Christmas a signal was sent round the ship which had come from admiralty. The "Australia" and "Sydney" will be ready to leave for Australia in the first week of April. Both ships will undergo eight weeks refit before leaving. You can imagine what an amount of excitement this caused. I sent you a Cable about it which I hope arrived alright.

The "Melbourne" is leaving sometime in February and will pick up the Destroyers on her way out.

On Christmas day the crew had a very joyous time. All officers who had anywhere to go went ashore. It was ordinary Sunday routine up till *eleven o clock, then the Admiral followed by as many officers that cared to go went round the mess deck. All the messes were gaily decorated with flags and green stuff. They all seemed very happy and were enjoying themselves. Some kind person in Australia had sent over an enormous load of apples and everyman had one, a great treat here where apples cost anything from sixpence each upwards.*

An impromptu band wandered round all day and when it got thirsty walked into one or other of the officers messes and stayed there banging away till mollified with beer.

After the admirals rounds the Gunroom visited the Wardroom and drank their health in champagne and ate Christmas cake, after which ceremony the wardroom did the likewise and visited us. Then we had dinner and anyone who could went ashore. I was on duty and in any case had nowhere to go. During the afternoon the ragtime band wandered round waking people out of their afternoon sleep and generally making a nuisance of them selves. I think that the festivities ought to have been kept till evening as things got very stale and all on board turned in early. Those ashore had a very good time I believe as Christmas Day is not a very important one in Scotland, the shops for most part carry on business as usual, their holiday being New Years Day.

The remainder of the week and up until New Year was spent in getting out Mess audits, that is of course when not on duty, and generally finishing off the year. I had to write up the monthly wine bill and get out the quarters wine audit as well as the ships fair log and several jobs for the Navigator. I am very glad I never went in for clerking, it took three days to do the wine quarterly and even then it did not balance, however Reilly who is now sub of the mess said he would fix it up for me as he does not go on leave until the 10th. Pedder the retiring sub of the mess is leaving the ship to go to Cambridge. All Dartmouth people who did not do full time at College are getting six months at Cambridge to finish their education. The official announcement also says that they are to generally have a good time which I think will be more than likely. The same is being done for all who left school to join the army only they go to Oxford. Uncle Rex has a great moan about it and I suppose you will not approve either.

On New Years Eve we had a very good time, mutual visits being paid by Ward room and Gun Room. During the evening a signal came through with a number of promotions and our Navigator has been promoted to Commander. I like him very much and so does everyone, he is coming out to Australia with the ship. At midnight the youngest snot rang sixteen bells and everyone sang Auld Lang Syne. We turned in about one o clock and I had to turn out again at five thirty to get my train south.

Four of us were to go by it and we somehow managed to dress and pack in time, then the boat was late in shoving off and we only caught the train by getting some men of a working party to carry our bags for us up to the station.

I got down to Leicester that evening and saw Enid for an hour. The next afternoon she had a day off so we went to a picture show and had dinner together. Enid is trying to get her four days Christmas leave about the nineteenth, in which case we will spend it in London however she may not get it as they are short handed and Enid is doing very senior work.

I spent a day in London which I had not intended to do but the Jersey boat was not running that night, so I paid a visit to Uncle Edward. He was very well or so seemed so and hard at work. London is very crowded and I had to get a shake down at my club, excuse the swank, the club is the Australian officers of which every Aussie officer is a member. I met an old school friend from Bathurst there, he has been in the flying corps for two years. The next evening I crossed over here from Weymouth. Shaw came with me as he has an uncle over here and wanted to see him. Everyone at the Manor is very well. There are two school friends of Guys staying here so we are quite a large party.

Your affectionate son
JohnMArmstrong

P.S. Ellie sends her love to you, and says you are to come over this side to take Enid back.

Australian Club
138 Picadilly
January 19th, 1919

Dear Dad

You will see by my address that I am back again in London. I spent a very enjoyable time at St Ouens altogether. During the last week it was rather bad weather and several outings had to be put off. On Wednesday some people came up to see Aunt Amy including Lady Wilson the Governors wife, A Russian fugitive princess and the Cox's. The Russian princess was quite celebrated.

Her father had been a Russian Prince, her mother an Italian princess and her husband an Austrian count, the latter was killed three months after the wedding. She herself had escaped from the

Bolshevics and at last taken refuge in Jersey. She would not talk of her adventures, and was very astounded at the way people discussed politics in England.

In the evening Ellie and I had dinner at the Vernons and afterwards went to a concert given by the St Peters people. There were songs and dancing, an amusing sketch and an operetta, it was quite good and Mrs Vernon was charming to us. The Next evening the St Ouens people went to the same show so I saw it twice. After the second show they sold numerous cakes by auction for some charity or other, it was great fun bidding but not quite so funny when you found yourself left with a rather stale cake at a good deal over shop price.

I left Jersey on Friday morning and met Enid late that evening at the Ivanhoe hotel where she had booked rooms. Next morning we got up at half past nine and I went to the bank.

There are a couple of men I know staying at the club but not as many Australian snots, the leave was too long and on their cash running out they decamped back to the ship. There is not much more news at present
Your affectionate son
JohnMArmstrong

HMAS "Australia"
January 27th 1919

At Sea
Dear Mother
To continue from my last letter. I got a message through to Enid last Sunday evening and she came down to London on Monday morning. It was jolly hard luck that she could not have had four days leave, it turned out if matron had known that I was also on leave Enid could quite easily have got her full time.

However, we made up for it as best we could on Monday afternoon. We went to see the "Luck of the Navy", a thrilling spy play in the afternoon and had dinner at Enid's club in the evening. My train left for the north at ten pm so I saw Enid back to her hotel and left myself an hour to catch the train and it was just as well I did as it was crowded from end to end, I by the merest luck got a seat but even then we were six in a carriage which held four in normal times. Jack Rayment had to sleep in the corridor and he got very cold.

Enid went back to her hospital next day, I think she is getting very fed up and wants to get home very badly. Even talks of breaking her contract if they are not demobilised within three months. I would not blame her at all if she did as there is very little real work to do at her hospital, most of the patients are quite well enough to leave the army only they will not demobilise them.

We all got back safely to the ship on Tuesday morning. Two snots whose money had given out had returned a week ago and were living a life of luxurious ease, occasionally taking on duties of officer of the watch but for the most part sitting round the Gunroom fire.

The weather has become quite cold and the woollens you sent me come in very handy.

The rest of the week was quite dull, just the usual routine.

Mr Franklin who used to be our maths instructor at College is the naval instructor in the Australia now. He arrived here about Christmas time. At first we were quite pleased with the change but now I rather think Mr Sheerer who used to take us knew more about his job, but then he was a genius.

On Saturday the freedom of the city of Edinburgh was given to Admiral Beatty. It was a very swell function I believe. There are rumours about that Beatty will resign the Command of the Grand Fleet soon and that Admiral Browning will get the job. In any case it will be a very diminished fleet. The First Fleet is to consist only of 13.5 inch ships and 15 inch ships, the others are to become second and third fleets which means that they remain in harbour all the time and only come out once a year or so.

On Sunday afternoon the "Australia" "Indomitable" "Inflexible" and "Sydney" left the Firth of Forth in company. The N.Z. had left a week ago. We manned ship and were cheered by all the Battle Cruisers on our way out. This morning we are steaming down the East coast of England and it is rather foggy. I have to go on the bridge now as the Navigator is up there.

Your affectionate son
JohnMArmstrong

HMS "Excellent"
February 4th 1919

Received 30th April, 1919
Dear Dad

You will see that I have changed my address. The "Excellent" is "Whale Island" in other words and here we are for a six weeks course. The first three weeks we will go to instruction everyday in the "Vernon" which is the torpedo school. And during the remainder of the time we will be doing Gunnery on the island.

To go back to the last week.

The "Indomitable", "Inflexible" and "Sydney" parted company off the mouth of the Thames and went on up to Chatham. The two battle cruisers are to go to 3rd fleet so I believe which means that they will swing round their moorings for the best part of the year and perhaps go to sea for an occasional jaunt just to keep the engines from rusting in. We ourselves are becoming quite ancient now days. They have four new Super Dreadnought Battle Cruisers ready for launching. They are the "Admiral" class and they are something to talk about I believe. The "Sydney" is to refit for our return to Australia.

By the way, what do you people think of President Wilson and his Yanks, we are getting rather fed up with him over here.

I used to have great arguments with Uncle Rex and Ellie about the Yanks and used to stick up for them but I have changed my mind now. Old Wilson comes over to the Peace Conference openly saying, that if he does not get what he wants U.S.A. will build a fleet to whip creation. In other words he is using Prussianism in just the same manner as the Huns would do. Anyone would think that America had done all the work of the war instead of just jumping on the right side at the latter part.

We got into Portsmouth harbour on Tuesday morning and moored to a buoy in mid stream. All day we got ammunition out of the ship and next morning went into No three basin where the ship still is. The "Melbourne" and the "Brisbane" are in the same basin, all preparing for a grand return to Australia. Things are not looking very bright just at present for the R.A.N. The R.N. have got their rise in pay and in consequence R.N. officers find no inducement in taking up a temporary billet in the R.A.N. when they get slightly better pay in the R.N. Then again Admiral Halsey wants to get as much as Admiral Patey got if he comes to Australia and the Navy Board don't want to give it. If they turned down Sir Lionel Halsey (one of the brainiest and cleverest men in the Service) they would get no other Admiral to take his place. Add to this that the Navy Board in Australia seems to be in a hopeless mix up and has well and truly got the wind up you will see that things do not look very bright.

Some of the snots went on leave on Thursday till Sunday but I did not for more reasons than one. Instead I loafed onboard and did no work whatsoever. On Sunday evening we packed our gear and came over here to Whale Island.

We have all got cabins and there are billiard rooms and sitting rooms etc, I fact the place is very much like a huge club. The Commander told us that so long as we behaved ourselves we could have whatever leave we liked and do practically as we wished. This morning was Monday and we went over to the "Vernon" after breakfast and began our Electrical course which will last a week. The Boat calls for us at lunchtime as we lunch at Whale Island and then takes us back to the "Vernon" again. We pack up at 3.30 and can then do what we like till midnight by which time we are supposed to be in the Island. However we do not generally stay up till that late hour.

Dinner is the one formal meal of the day.

The Island is not very full just at present. There is a "long course" of R.N. Lieuts and a certain number of R.N.R. and R.N.V.R. people beside ourselves.

Your affectionate son
JohnMArmstrong

HMS "Excellent"
February 9th 1919

Received 30th April, 1919
Dear Mother

Here we are at the end of our first week's course in the "Vernon". The work has been on electricity and although it is mostly revision of work we have done on board it has been very interesting. Our working hours are from 9.AM till 11.30 and 1PM till 3.30. We return to Whale Island for lunch and again for tea. After tea we can do what we like, play billiards, read, go to sleep or go ashore. We have standing leave from 3.30 till 7.30 and if we wish it can get up till midnight by asking the Commander.

The "Vernon" is composed of three old hulks of about Nelsons time which are moored head and a stern between a couple of mud flats in Portsmouth harbour. "Vernon 1" is the residential ship where officers, instructors and men under instruction live, and "Vernon 11 and 111" are full of the latest torpedo and electrical devices in the service. The "Vernon" has a varied collection both of distinguished officers and interesting curios.

Among the instructing officers are some of the inventors of our most modern appliances and you also run across old dug outs who still talk about the first iron-clads.

There is one officer whom we have run into who is of special interest. He is a Lieutenant Commander Harrison R.N.V.R. and at the outbreak of war he was working with a German inventor in England, on searchlights. At the outbreak of war the German was interned and they very kindly gave him permission to carry on with his work, he rather naturally refused and Harrison pinched his ideas, improved on them and gave us a searchlight far in advance of any the Germans had.

Among the curios are German torpedoes of all marks. They seem to have turned out a standard torpedo which could be made cheaply and in sufficient numbers to keep the U. Boats well supplied.

I met a Lieutenant Lacey here who is doing the Long course for Gunnery lieutenant. On hearing we were Australians he asked me did I know Armadale, and if so did I know the Tindalls. He had been to several dances at Fir Grove quite lately. Portsmouth is a pretty dull sort of place. I went to a theatre last week but it was very provincial after London theatres.

We are busy getting uniforms before leaving England, and have so far managed to get Round Jackets and dirks out of the Naval Representative. It is rather a waste giving us Round Jackets and even dirks I think. We will only use them for six months or at least we hope it will only be for six months. I have to get a complete new outfit of white uniform as well, as my old whites are too small now, and if I can run to it I will get a new blue uniform as well but they cost £ 8 a suit and my exchequer is none too high just at present; The fault of having such a lot of leave lately.

Sorry there is not more news for you. I am only just beginning to realise that we will be home again in three months time. Although events have moved quickly it seems a long time since we left on the 18th January, 1918.

> *Your affectionate son*
> *JohnMArmstrong*

> HMS "Excellent"
> Portsmouth
> February 24th 1919

Received 30th April, 1919
Dear Dad

We finished our Torpedo course on Friday and on the whole we did rather well, – Though I says it as shouldn't – as it was not a regular course we did not have any fixed exams to pass at the end, however they gave us one to see if we had been awake and everyone got over 80%. – I got 87% and the top man got 94%, certainly it was an easy test but all these things are noted down both in Melbourne and at the Admiralty so on the whole we were rather pleased with ourselves. The work was intensely interesting especially as some of the officers, – or rather I should say one in particular, – who took us, had just come from the Harwich Force where he had been during most of the war. The Harwich Force are the "Knuts" at destroyer work, even more so than the "Dover Patrol".

They have been in constant touch with the enemy all through and what they do not know about light craft work is not worth knowing. So as you can imagine how interested we all were especially as it is the aim of all right minded snotties to be sent to light craft on getting their stripe.

The Navy Board has just bought six new Destroyers and six "J" class submarines and things are looking up in that direction. However to balance it they have made a mess of the higher commands and Admiral Halsey may not be coming out with us. I think that he is the man to get out in Australia, he would set the whole show on a sound basis but the Politicians know that he is a good man and that he would not countenance their usual tricks so they don't want him there. Their ideal is some nice kind old dugout who might be very fine at spit and polish but who would not disturb their Pockets or think of organising the R.A.N. in a rational manner. If Admiral Halsey goes it means that Captain James and Commander North would go too as they form what is generally know as a family party.

All our year and the year senior to us are going out with the Australian fleet. They have built gunrooms in the Sydney and Melbourne for our crowd and the senior term replace RN subs in the destroyer and submarines.

The "Melbourne" leaves on the 28th of this month, she is to "mother" numerous destroyers out and then join us at Port Albany.

There is to be a big dance at the Town Hall next Wednesday given by all Australian sailors, all the officers are invited and it ought to be rather fun.

The N.Z. with admiral Jellicoe leaves in a couple of days and if programmes are carried out we are to meet her at Port Albany some time in May, we are all to leave here on the 8th April and arrive in Australia towards the end of May, do a tour of the Australian Capitals and moor up in Farm Cove about the 2nd week in June and I most heartily hope it will be so. This climate is just a little too cold for me.

I am sending you some photos taken just before we left the Firth of Forth, that is all except the "Germans" which were taken at the surrender.

Your affectionate son
JohnMArmstrong

Midshipman John Malet Armstrong (1900-1988)

HMS "Excellent"
March 2nd 1919

Received 20th May, 1919

Dear Mother

Just had an enormous Australian mail, the last came just over two months ago so you can imagine that it was well appreciated.

I am glad my Christmas cards proved a success and that the cable arrived up to time.

The new lot of Australian snotties seem to have had a good time before they left; I see young Wills is not on the list, rather a good thing too.

Captain Grant has left the College as I suppose you know, I think it was a pity he ever became Captain, he was just the man as Commander but as Captain he hardly knew what to do with himself.

We have heard definitely that Admiral Halsey is not going to take over as C in C. Australian fleet and it is rumoured that Commodore Dumaresque will take over. He has been Captain of the "Sydney" for some time and is a great inventor of Gunnery instruments.

Another rumour is that the Australian Navy is to get a 21% rise of pay. Good luck to it. The worst of it is that R.A.N. snotties are considered to have more pay than is good for them at present so I don't think we will be included. If it comes out the rise will bring us into line with the proposed rise in R.N. pay which is 100% for senior officers and 85% for Lieutenants and below.

Our first week at Gunnery instruction ended quite happily. We have been doing rifle and field Exercises, field gun drill etc. At first we had to do half an hours drill before breakfast but this was remitted after our third day in consideration for progress made, so we are feeling rather bucked. At Divisons this morning the Gunnery Commander told the Captain that we were progressing entirely to his satisfaction.

Mr Darley was down here last week-end. He is leaving shortly for Australia to set up the new Gunnery school at Westernport where he hopes to see us within the next nine months or so.

As far as we know our exams will not be postponed in which case we will sit for them some time in August; We are all very pleased to have got in our Torpedo and Gunnery courses and the fellows who were in the "Agincourt" and "Canada" say we have stolen a march on them. The "Melbourne" left on the 27th of last month, she is to escort numerous destroyers out, via Singapore. All the Agincourt's snotties went in her so they will be the first to arrive back in Aussie. They were all crammed into an enlarged cabin hastely constructed and ironically called a Gunroom.

Sixteen the Gunroom has to hold and it is about the size of a Captains cabin in a light cruiser. I don't envy then their trip through the tropics.

Enid is doing her best to get demobilised but it seems doubtful if she will be able to get a passage for some time. What a pity it was that Dad could not get over here.

I see by the papers that "Flu" has broken out again in Sydney, I wonder did you and Dad get your proposed trip to Tasmania.

Good-bye for the present, I ought to arrive about a month or five weeks after this letter, which fact has been the cause of people breaking into unseemly mirth at all sorts of odd times and places.

Your affectionate son
JohnMArmstrong

HMS Excellent
Portsmouth
March 9th 1919

Received 20th May 1919
Dear Dad

We have finished our field training course now and begin a weeks Lewis gun tomorrow. The first week of Field training was quite severe, we had a loud voiced chief Petty officer as a drill instructor and he made us hop around to some tune. However he relented in the second week and we spent most of it at rifle shooting and revolver practice which was much more to our liking. We had no exam at the end of the course as we are only putting in time, however it will help enormously when we pass for subs.

The "Canada" fellows have been appointed to the "Sydney" and I believe have just joined her at Chatham. They will have plenty of time to settle down in her; the snots in the "Melbourne" had to join in such a hurry that many of them left their chests behind. The fellows senior to us are being appointed to our destroyers and submarines so that the first two years to pass out of Jervis Bay are all going home again, and very pleased to get home again we will be.

None of us like the English climate, it is not so much the cold as the continual rain and slush that we object too.

I hear that the new lot of Australian snots are to arrive here within the next two weeks, Whale Island will take them in hand and remove all the after effects of their long voyage. We are wondering where they will be sent to as to all intents the R.N. do not want junior officers, in fact they are offering inducements to junior officers to retire from the service. Strikes are very thick here just at present, I have come to the conclusion that Australia is not so bad as she is painted with regards to strikes, this country is just as bad if not worse. The miners seem to have a sound grievance but they overdo the thing by a long way. They are trying to rush the Government into nationalization of all key industries by threatening to strike at a critical period, in fact they and the transport workers and railwaymen want to govern the country. Sorry there is not much news just now, adieu till the end of May.

Your affectionate son
JohnMArmstrong

HMS Excellent
Portsmouth
March 16th 1919

Received 20th May 1919
Dear Mother

Many thanks for your letters and birthday wishes, a mail has just come in bringing letters from both you and Dad. I am very glad to hear that you got away on your Tasmanian trip, it must have been a great change for you.

Our course at Whale Island finished yesterday and we could all have gone on three weeks leave, however half a dozen of us myself included found pressing reasons for not going on leave for any length of time and here we are doing an extra weeks gunnery control.

My pressing reason is a Uniform bill. All my white uniforms are two or three sizes too small for me and I wanted another blue uniform as well and as the blue uniforms cost £8-3 and the whites come to £ 10 I thought it as well to economise.

All our old officers have left the "Australia" at least all except one or two and there is some body appointed to the ship almost every day. Admiral Halsey is definitely not going. Commodore Dumaresque takes command of the fleet and Rear Admiral Grant is to be first Naval Member in Australia, all we want now is a Captain and Commander. I don't know how they are going to man the new ships that England has given us, we are short as it is and then many of the men are applying to leave the service on returning to Australia.

It is not long to wait now, another three weeks ought to see us clear of England and five weeks after that we are due at Albany. At Albany we are to pick up the New Zealand and carry on to Sydney staying some time in Melbourne on the way. The new lot of snots are due to arrive next Wednesday, I hope they enjoy themselves for the next two years over here.

I am going on leave some time after next week to say good bye to people and to spend a couple of days with Enid. I don't know when she will be going back. Transport seems to be very short.

Your affectionate son

JohnMArmstrong

HMAS Australia
May 22nd 1919
At sea

Received 25th August 1919

Dear Dad

I will make this a history of events since just before we left England. When our course at Whale Island was finished we were given ten days leave and were to be onboard by the 1st April, the ship being expected to sail on the 5th. I was rather short of cash at the time so with half a dozen others I did another week at Whale Island. During this last week the new lot of snotties arrived. They were dumped in the island while waiting for appointments and forthwith got a good shaking up. We being few in numbers compared with the others got mixed up in the shaking process and were rather pleased when our time ended.

I went up to Leicester for three days and said goodbye to Enid. She expected to hear some more about her passage out within a short time. She sends all sorts of messages to you and mother and is looking forward to a general reunion as soon as she can possibly do it.

On the way back to Portsmouth I stayed a night in London and went to see Mrs Bray and Miss Austin. Ken was spending the evening with them, he was over for a weeks leave; wasn't it luck that I should run into him like that? His unit was in Belgium but he did not know its future movements. When we got back to the ship on the 1st it was only to find that the date of sailing had been put back to the 15th and we got another nine days leave. I drew some pay and went over to Jersey with Shaw; he has relations in the island. The people at the manor were very well, Guy has not quite recovered from his heart yet but is well on the way. I had quite a gay time there, a couple of small dances and numerous outings. The Coxes are thinking of settling down in the island. I also met Fred Le Gros, he seemed rather bored with life except when Vallery Cox was on the horizon. Everyone sends you innumerable messages and want to know when you and mother are to pay another visit to their part of the world.

When at last I got back to the ship she had just been painted inside and out in preparation for the Prince of Wales' visit. The last three days in Pompey the ship was thrown open to inspection and numerous receptions were held on board. The Prince came onboard on Wednesday 25th. He shook hands with all the officers and inspected all the men. Then he read a message from the King and Joe Cook got up and replied in his best preaching manner. The Prince then inspected the "Brisbane" and returned onboard to lunch. After lunch everyone had their photos taken and the Prince went off. He made himself extremely popular with everybody onboard. That day we had fifteen Admirals onboard from Sir R. Wemyss down.

On the 17th we shoved off from the Railway Pier, Portsmouth at 8. AM and proceeded to Spit Head, the "Brisbane" was already there having left harbour on the 16th. At noon we left Spit Head with the Brisbane in company and rounding the Isle of White set course for the Ushant at 15 knots. The Bay of Biscay let us down very lightly and on the 20th we passed the Straights of Gibraltar and went alongside the mole of Gib harbour. While at sea we snotties kept watches and during the day do instruction. But at Gibraltar Captain Cumberledge excused us all duties and gave us permission to go ashore and see the sights. A party of us went up the Rock and saw the galleries in the morning and in the afternoon a party went to Algeciras the Spanish town to see a bull fight which did not come off. The rest of us had a bathe and a sunbathe, the first since January 18. All the men got leave and there were not a few scraps with the men from some Yank ships. Next day the 22nd we shoved off and set course for Malta. The trip was quite uneventful and we made Valetta harbour on Anzac Day. The harbour is very like a dolls harbour and is very picturesque, rather after the style of Sydney harbour on a small scale though the shore is nothing like "our harbour". The "Sydney" and our six submarines with their depot ship were in harbour so the Australian flag was very much in evidence. We were only in harbour for twelve hours but I got ashore in the afternoon and had a look round the town. It is not much of a place except for its harbour. The houses in many parts are falling to pieces and a hot white glare is over everything.

I bought some Malta lace, most of which was pinched. I think the man who sold it to me abstracted a lot while making up the parcel. That evening we left Malta and set a course for Port Said. It began to get fairly hot nearing Egypt and we went into all whites. The ship arrived at Port Said on Monday 27th, a blazing hot day. As soon as the ship was secured numbers of coal barges covered with yelling niggers came alongside and we were able to watch the pleasing spectacle of someone else coaling for us. All who could went ashore at once to get away from the heat and coal dust. On landing the usual crowd of niggers came up anxious to sell anything from a putty medal to a suit of clothes. The shops were not up to much I thought, their keepers look on all Australians with suspicion, clearly another case of spoiling the Egyptians. We could have got free train passes to Cairo although it was against orders owing to the disturbances, however we did not think it worth while as it meant fourteen hours in the train and only about five hours there.

In the evening the mataloes went ashore and proceeded to make things lively, the Australian soldiers giving a helping hand.

The disturbances on the Nile have not effected Port Said much, still the native quarter is not a pleasant place at night, as a party of four lieutenants found out. They drove out in a Garry and the driver refused to take them back under a fiver. One of them had a six shooter with him which finally persuaded the driver to be reasonable.

Next morning at seven we slipped and proceeded with a pilot into the canal. All along the first part of the canal we were escorted by Diggers on motor bicycles. About noon the ship passed Kantara a large Australian camp at the point where the Palestine railway crosses the canal. The banks were lined with Australian soldiers who passed many a lurid remark about Billy Hughes and hotly demanded when they were going home and was Billy on board; " no 'es not on board" came back the answer "we ditched 'im back in the Atlantic". After that everyone cheered. About four o clock we passed another large digger camp at Ismalia and the same thing was gone through again. Dusk fell as we were passing the bitter lakes and we switched on our searchlights. Much language was expended when the lights failed which was fairly often.

We reached Suez about midnight and came to on anchor some distance from the town. Next day nobody could go ashore owing to the town being quarantined. A party of snotties visited the Australian troop ship Dorset and much to our indignation were recalled to write up the theory of tides.

At midday on the 29th we sailed from Suez just as the "Sydney" and submarines arrived. The "Brisbane" had engine trouble so we proceeded alone into the sweltering Red Sea

(I have come to the end of my pad and as this is too thin to continue on the back I will use some note paper)

The Red Sea quite lived up to its reputation for heat, making everyone bad tempered. To make matters worse the Egyptians in Port Soudan thought a change of Government would be to their liking and we were kept going at slow speed so as not to be too far away if we were wanted. At last on Sunday 4th we passed Perim Island and made direct for Aden which rightly deserves its name of the "Last place God made". We anchored about three miles from the landing place and proceeded to coal, or rather, be coaled by yelling niggers. We stayed at Aden for five days while various courts of enquiry and a court martial was held. The Governor of the place gave a hop, which we returned.

One day half the Gunroom went away cutter sailing and came back the colour of Beetroot. The remainder of our fleet trickled into port after us and left again before us so that all the way to Colombo we were passing H.M.A. ships. Half way we picked up submarine J9 and towed her for two days as to rest her engines. We got to Colombo on the 14th. The Brisbane was in before us and the others came in next day. We were again coaled by niggers and all officers who could went to Kandy, unfortunately I could not get the time. Colombo is another place the Australians have spoilt. Things there are three or four times as dear as they were before the war. Jack Rayment and I did an afternoon round trip in rickshaws seeing a Bhuddist temple, the Cinamon gardens etc. An Australian mail met us at Colombo but I did not get any letters, I think that letters have missed us to a large extent arriving at Portsmouth after we left.

The "Australia" left Colombo on the 18th, the other ships were to remain there some time owing to damage in the submarines.

The voyage to Freemantle was quite uneventful. Neptune came aboard when we crossed the line and initiated all and sundry including the Commodore and Captain into the most noble order of Sea Urchins.

Games and sports were got up in which the Gunroom did quite well. The boxing was the best part of it but owing to a heavy swell in the latter part of the run it has not been finished yet.

We got in here at 6.30 this morning and have been coaling all day so I think I will say goodnight. We arrive in Sydney about the 18th or 20th of June.

A Bientot

JohnMArmstrong

Thus ends Jock's time in the Great War on HMAS Australia.

POSTSCRIPT

Jock was to go on to many greater adventures of daring in World War 2, becoming Captain of HMAS Australia, the County class cruiser (Kent subclass). He won the DSO and US Navy Cross for his actions commanding the ship at the Battle of Lingayen in the Philippines in January, 1945, when the ship was hit by five Japanese kamikazes. He was also awarded the CBE and finished his career as Commodore and 2nd member of the Australian Navy Board, the first member being Admiral John Collins.

Jock's friend Jack Rayment died as a Commander on HMAS Australia on October 21st, 1944 when a Japanese plane hit the bridge of the ship killing its Captain Emile Dechaineux and wounding Commodore John Collins. Jock who was in New Guinea took over as Captain.

Jock retired to Jersey in 1962 with his wife Philippa Marett (of La Haule

Jock as Captain HMAS Australia, January 1945 (David Armstrong)

Manor) and they lived at La Mielle at La Mielle House, La Route de La Haule, St Brelade. He died on December 30th, 1988, aged 88 and is buried in the Marett family grave in St Brelade's Churchyard. They had three children: Professor David Malet (1926-2014),Philip (1927-2013) and Suzanne Dumaresq (1929 - and his four grandchildren.

I am saddened that I never met Jock or Philippa in their retirement in Jersey.

Jock & Philippa's Gravestone on Marett plot, St Brelade's Churchyard, Jersey (author)

SOURCES

The letters and certain photographs as noted are reproduce with kind permission of the National Library of Australia, Canberra – papers of John Malet Armstrong – MS 9675

BV - #0005 - 290322 - C18 - 229/152/10 - PB - 9781908336460 - Gloss Lamination